CONCEPTS AND INQUIRY:
The Educational Research Council
Social Science Program

The Human Adventure

The Interaction of Cultures

Prepared by the Social Science Staff of the Educational
Research Council of America

ALLYN AND BACON, INC.

Boston   Rockleigh, N.J.   Atlanta   Dallas   Belmont, Calif.

THE HUMAN ADVENTURE SERIES WAS PREPARED BY THE FOLLOWING MEMBERS OF THE SOCIAL SCIENCE STAFF OF THE EDUCATIONAL RESEARCH COUNCIL OF AMERICA:

NANCY BOSTICK, CONSTANCE BURTON, NANCY HENDERSON, MICHAEL JOYCE, MARILYN McLAUGHLIN, AGNES MICHNAY, JAMES PACKARD, MARIE RICHARDS, MARY RITLEY, JUDITH WENTZ, MARLENE ZWEIG.

MARY CATHERINE McCARTHY, EDITOR-IN-CHIEF

RAYMOND ENGLISH, DIRECTOR

The Educational Research Council of America acknowledges the contributions of the Kettering Family Fund and the Martha Holden Jennings Foundation, which have made possible the Social Science Program of the Educational Research Council of America.

Cover by Barry Zaid, Push Pin Studios, Inc.

Title page photo Courtesy of the Library of Congress.

CONTENTS

MAPS

ACKNOWLEDGMENTS

Preface — facing page one, Musée des Tissus, Lyon, Andre Gamet — Rapho Guillumette; **Chapter 1** — page 6, Library of Congress; p. 9, The Bodleian Library, Oxford, England; p. 11, Courtesy of the Smithsonian Institution, Freer Gallery of Art, Washington, D.C.; p. 13, Peabody Museum, Salem, Mark Sexton; p. 15, 17, Yenching Institute, Harvard University; p. 20, (both) Courtesy of the National Gallery of Art, Washington, D.C.; p. 23, 26, Radio Times Hulton Picture Library, London, England; **Chapter 2** — p. 28, Peabody Museum, Salem; p. 31, Peabody Museum, Salem, Mark Sexton; p. 32, Library of Congress; p. 34, National Maritime Museum, Greenwich, England; p. 36, 40, Peabody Museum, Salem, Mark Sexton; **Chapter 3** — p. 42, Courtesy of the Smithsonian Institution, Freer Gallery of Art, Washington, D.C.; p. 44, Courtesy of Mr. and Mrs. Nasli Heeramaneck, photo by Barney Burstein; p. 45, Courtesy of the Victoria and Albert Museum, London, England, Derek Roe; p. 47, (both) Peabody Museum, Salem, Mark Sexton; p. 50, Culver Pictures, Inc.; p. 51, (both) Doranne Jacobson — Editorial Photocolor Archives, Inc.; p. 53, Radio Times Hulton Picture Library, London, England; p. 54, The Bettmann Archives, Inc.; p. 55, Radio Times Hulton Picture Library, London, England; p. 57, Culver Pictures, Inc.; **Chapter 4** — p. 58, Mark and Evelyne Bernheim — Rapho Guillumette; p. 61, (all) Jacques Jangoux; p. 62, 63, Courtesy of the Trustees of the British Museum; p. 64, National Palace, Mexico; p. 66, 67, 70, Library of Congress; p. 71, 74, Radio Times Hulton Picture Library, London, England; **Chapter 5** — p. 75 (top) Harrison Forman, (bottom) Erik Verg — Globe Photos, Inc.; p. 86, 89, from *Journal of the Discovery of the Source of the Nile* by J. H. Speke, London, 1863; p. 90, Brown Brothers; p. 92, National Bank of India Limited, London, England; p. 94, 96, Marc and Evelyne Bernheim — Rapho Guillumette; **Chapter 6** — p. 106, Historical Picture Service; p. 109, Sovfoto; p. 112, (left) The Bettmann Archives, Inc.; p. 117, The Phillips Collection, Washington, D.C.; p. 119, 120, Culver Pictures, Inc.; p. 124, (both) Library of Congress; p. 126, Sadahide, *A Foreign Merchant's Building in Yokohama*, Courtesy of the Emily Crane Chadbourne Collection, Art Institute of Chicago; **Chapter 7** — p. 128, Larry Rivers, *Dying and Dead Veteran*, Courtesy of Tibor de Nagy Gallery, New York City, Barney Burstein; p. 131, Museo Nacional de Historia, Chapultepec Castle, Mexico; p. 137, Culver Pictures, Inc.; p. 139, Courtesy of the American Antiquarian Society; p. 141, (left) Harry T. Peters Collection, Museum of the City of New York, (right) Collection of Edgar William and Bernice Chrysler Garbisch (detail); p. 145, (left) New York Historical Society; **Conclusion** — p. 150, Lyonel Feininger, *Marktkirch in Halle*, Nere Pinakothek and Neue Staatsgalerie, Munich, Germany from European Art Color — Peter Adelberg, New York City; p. 160, Ben Shahn, *Italian Landscape II*, Courtesy Collection of Mr. and Mrs. Erving Levick, Buffalo, New York, Barney Burstein.

All photos not otherwise credited are the work of Allyn and Bacon staff photographers.

Illustrations and Charts: Len Ebert, pp. 3, 81, 83, 87, 103, 155, 158; Contis Studios, pp. 68, 83, 87, 163.

Map design and compilation by Allyn and Bacon.

A NOTE TO STUDENTS

To help you find out things for yourself and to use the things you know, think about the problems and questions as you read. They are marked ▶, ●, or ★.

These symbols mean:

- ▶ easy to solve
- ● harder to solve — more thinking is needed
- ★ something extra — usually requires research

Many words in this book are respelled to help you pronounce them. The key below will help you read the respellings.

a	hat, cap	j	jam, enjoy	u	cup, butter
ā	age, face	k	kind, seek	u̇	full, put
ã	care, air	l	land, coal	ü	rule, move
ä	father, far	m	me, am	ū	use, music
		n	no, in		
b	bad, rob	ng	long, bring	v	very, save
ch	child, much			w	will, woman
d	did, red	o	hot, rock	y	young, yet
		ō	open, go	z	zero, breeze
e	let, best	ô	order, all	zh	measure, seizure
ē	equal, be	oi	oil, voice		
er	term, learn	ou	house, out	ə	represents:
					a in about
f	fat, if	p	paper, cup		e in taken
g	go, bag	r	run, try		i in April
h	he, how	s	say, yes		o in lemon
		sh	she, rush		u in circus
i	it, pin	t	tell, it		
ī	ice, five	th	thin, both		
		ŦH	then, smooth		

From THORNDIKE-BARNHART JUNIOR DICTIONARY by E. L. Thorndike and Clarence L. Barnhart. Copyright © 1968 by Scott, Foresman and Company.

The Dominance of Western Culture

All over the world, the nineteenth century was a time of swift change. So many important things happened that we cannot try to study them all. In this book we shall pay attention to a few things that are still very important today.

The nineteenth century was a time when Western European civilization took the position of leadership in the world. Western ideas and ways of life had spread to other countries. Western trade and government had spread, also.

The beginnings of Western European leadership started in the sixteenth century. Western ideas were spread through exploration, colonization, conquest, and trade. They moved to the New World. Through Russia, they moved into central Asia. Western culture came to other parts of Asia. It came to Australia, New Zealand, and the islands of the Pacific. In the end it had great influence in the "cradle of civilization" — the Middle East — and the land where the human race began — the continent of Africa.

- Review the changes that brought Western European leadership in the sixteenth and seventeenth centuries.

- What other great civilizations existed in the sixteenth century?

Persian artisans were also affected by Western influence.

1

By the nineteenth century, Western civilization seemed so powerful that other cultures and civilizations looked as if they would all be **Westernized**. This meant that other countries would copy the culture and ideas of the West. Some of these countries were also ruled by Western European countries. We call this great power of the West the **dominance** of Western civilization. It even looked as if Western Europe would rule the world.

Those days are gone. Yet even today we find Western ideas and Western technology nearly everywhere. This spreading of Western civilization seems to be the most important of all the controlling ideas in the nineteenth century.

What happened, however, was really more important than just the spread of Western culture. What happened was a great **interaction of cultures**. Western men and ideas came to non-Western cultures. This contact of Western culture with non-Western culture had great effects on the world. Western ways of life and Western people did not just dominate other cultures. They stirred non-Western people into action. They started new movements of nationalism. They led to revolutions. People everywhere began to look for change. They began to want industry and science. They began to want to govern themselves. They began to study their own cultures. They began to resist the power of the West.

▶ Make sure that you know what these words mean: *civilization, culture, non-Western cultures, domination.*

● What are the main things you need to know in order to study and understand a culture?

Imperialism

What form did Western domination take in the nineteenth century? Historians sum it up in the word **imperialism**. Imperialism comes from the same root as *empire*. Imperialism occurs whenever a strong society rules over or controls weaker societies. This is not new. From the first civilization onward, empires have been built, empires have grown, empires have fallen, and new empires have risen. The Sumerians, the Babylonians, the Assyrians, the

Egyptians, the Hittites, the Greeks, the Romans, the Persians, the Muslim Arabs, the Chinese, the Maya, the Aztecs, the Mongols, and many other peoples built empires. They were all imperialistic. Yet there was never quite so huge a burst of imperialism as came from Western Europe in the Modern Age.

Culture Contact

Imperialism helped to bring about the meeting of people and ideas from many different cultures. This is part of a process called

culture contact. By this we mean the things that happen when one culture or way of life comes into close touch with another and different culture.

Culture contact can bring bad or good or mixed bad and good results. Its worst result is genocide (jen′ə sīd). **Genocide** means the killing of a people and their culture.

Another possible result is acculturation (ə kul′ chər ā′ shən). The word **acculturation** describes the effect of the contact between an underdeveloped society and a more advanced one. Thus, acculturation also describes the new culture that grows out of culture contact. Acculturation usually means that the dominant, controlling culture takes over and changes the weaker culture. The people of the weaker culture accept the dominant culture in place of their own. Acculturation usually means, too, that the dominant culture takes some ideas and ways of living from the culture it replaces.

Another result may be **segregation** (seg′ rə gā′ shən). This means that the people of the weaker culture are forced to live separated (or segregated) from the people of the dominant culture. They may, for example, be kept in *reservations.*

Culture contact may also result in a **pluralistic** (plür′ əl is′ tik) society, in which peoples with different cultures live side by side. The British rulers of India, for example, tried to keep peace between Hindus and Muslims. The rulers did not try to change or favor either culture group. Another type of pluralistic society is found in the United States. Here we find a common American culture, but many different **subcultures** (sub′kul′ chərz) living together inside the larger culture.

- Look up the meaning of *subcultures.* Name some examples of subcultures found in the United States.

- Make sure you know the meaning of *genocide, acculturation, segregation*, and *pluralistic* society. Can you give examples of each of these types of culture contact?

★ Find the meaning of *assimilation* and *apartheid.* Which types of culture contact do they fit into?

- Why does culture contact often present big problems?

In the pages that follow, we shall study examples of imperialism and of culture contact.

Some Controlling Ideas of the West

What were the big ideas that spread with Western civilization? The root ideas were the mixture of Judeo-Christian and Greco-Roman ideas that we have discussed many times.

▶ What were these two sets of ideas? Why did they make Western European culture *restless*?

● What "new" controlling ideas grew up in Western Europe in the sixteenth, seventeenth, and eighteenth centuries?

If you answered the last question correctly, you will know the big ideas that spread with Western civilization. Among the most important were certain values and political ideas. As we read, we will study more about some of these controlling ideas.

For example, *nationalism* was the idea that people of the same nation should be united in one state. *Democracy* meant that all men should share in the government. *Representation* was the method by which men could share in government. *Freedom* and *equality* were two ideas with many different meanings. Yet, these two ideas were very important to most Westerners. Many Westerners believed in *progress*. Progress was the idea that things could change for the better. Some of these ideas led to the idea of *revolution*.

Western societies did not always live up to these ideas. Yet the ideas were very strong. They went all over the world. As people from non-Western cultures learned about the West, they also learned these ideas. Then they began to use them.

● What different meanings of *freedom* and *equality* do you know?

● Many Western thinkers disagreed about *progress* and *revolution*. What do we call those who think that change will usually be for the better? What do we call those who think that change and revolution are often dangerous?

▶ What are some of the types of revolution you know?

chapter 1

Chinese Imperialism Under the Manchus

Introduction: Imperialism

As we have seen, imperialism is the control of one people or nation over another. This control may be political or economic or both. It may be the result of warfare, or trade, or exploration, or colonization. It is not a new idea. Empires have been built since the beginning of early civilizations. Throughout history, imperialism has taken many forms.

In some areas it took the form of colonization. **Colonization** is the movement of *settlers* or *colonists* to new areas. Colonization often happens in lands with few or no native inhabitants. It sometimes happens in lands which already have many inhabitants. Then the native inhabitants have to make way for the colonists. The interests of the native inhabitants are often ignored. Colonization was the pattern of Western imperialism in the New World, in Australia and New Zealand, and in South Africa.

Another form of imperialism is **conquest and rule**. Sometimes this comes as the result of warfare. The imperial power does not allow colonists to drive out the native inhabitants. Instead, it governs the people, taxes them, and opens up trade with them. Conquest and rule was the pattern of Western imperialism in many places. It happened in India, in Southeast Asia, in much of Africa, and in most of the small islands of the Pacific. Sometimes a certain amount of colonization went along with the conquest and rule. This happened in Kenya (in East Africa) and in Algeria (in North Africa).

Sometimes imperialism took the form of protectorates (prə tek′ tər its). A **protectorate** is a land under the protection of an imperial power. The imperial power allows the native government to go on ruling the people. However, the imperial power takes over the defense of the land and expects taxes and trade in return. Protectorates were found in Africa, the Middle East, and in parts of India.

There is also **economic imperialism**. In this case, the imperial power does not conquer or govern. It simply uses its power to force a country to trade with it. Trade and money lead to control of the economic life of the country. This was the story of Western imperialism in China. The United States carried out economic imperialism in Latin America.

The different forms of imperialism often overlapped. For example, conquest and rule also meant that the imperial power dominated the economic life of the conquered people. In addition, all forms of imperialism usually meant some **cultural imperialism**. That is, the culture of the imperial power affected the native culture. Many times the original inhabitants were forced to accept the way of life of the imperialist power.

▸ Which empire that you have studied would you choose to show *conquest and rule* imperialism? Which would you choose to show *colonization*? Why?

● Colonists often turned against imperialism. They became *anti-imperialistic*. So did conquered peoples. What do you think would be the difference between these two sorts of anti-imperialism?

We are going to look at examples of Western and non-Western imperialism. Western Europeans expanded into many parts of

This picture is from Marco Polo's book of world travels. His writing about the Chinese court of Kublai Khan in 1271 helped Europeans to learn more about the great empires to the East.

the world. They crossed the oceans in their ships. They discovered lands which had never had contact with the West. Western Europeans brought their goods and their ideas to these lands. They caused important changes in the cultures of these lands. As time passed, they established an imperial control over many people. We shall study Western imperialism in China, India, and Africa.

Before we examine Western imperialism, however, we shall study an example of non-Western imperialism. The example is China. The Chinese expanded overland during the Manchu dynasty. They conquered neighboring states and made these states part of China. The Manchus created a huge empire. They made China safe from land invasion. They also sealed China off from contact with the outside world.

As we read about these examples of imperialism, we should keep the following questions in mind:

Why did imperialists try to extend their control over other lands? What things attracted them?

How did the imperialists gain control over other lands? Why were they able to succeed?

In what ways did foreign control hurt the dominated people? In what ways did it help them?

China Before the Manchus

After its conquest by Genghis Khan, China was ruled by the Mongols. This period, which lasted from 1260 to 1368, was called the **Yuan** (yü än) **dynasty**. It reached its most powerful point in the reign of Kublai Khan. Marco Polo visited Kublai Khan's court and stayed for 25 years. When he returned to Europe, he brought news of the wonderful civilization of China. Europeans later were eager to trade for Chinese silks, porcelain, and tea. They admired Chinese culture and Chinese products very much.

- Review what you have learned about the Mongols. What happened to Mongol power after Kublai Khan?

- Why was Western Europe eager to trade with China? What was taking place in Western Europe around this time?

After years of Mongol rule, the Chinese led a successful revolt against the Yuan dynasty. The leader of the rebellion made himself emperor. He called himself the first emperor of the **Ming dynasty**. Political power was returned to the Chinese themselves. The Ming dynasty began in 1368 and lasted nearly 300 years.

The Ming dynasty was generally a time of peace and prosperity. The first Ming emperors were strong rulers. They made the empire much larger. Many splendid buildings were put up. Great works of art were produced.

▶ Make sure you know what *dynasty* means.

Decline of the Ming Dynasty

After many years, the power of the Ming dynasty began to decline. The last emperor was weak, and his officials were not honest. Taxes were high. Crops failed and famine spread through the provinces. Border invasions increased. Local rulers were unable to govern the angry and unhappy people. Peasants began to rebel. Many of China's territories and tribute states grew strong enough to break away from the empire. The Chinese Empire began to fall apart.

To the Chinese people, these misfortunes were a sign that the Ming dynasty had lost the **Will of Heaven**.

This Ming landscape shows the traditional Chinese view of man as a small part of the world of nature.

▶ What did the Chinese mean by the *Will of Heaven*?

● Why was it difficult for a ruler to keep power when his people thought he had lost the Will of Heaven?

As the Chinese Empire became weaker, the nomadic tribes who lived on the northern steppes became stronger. The **Manchu** tribes had been united into a powerful kingdom. They had already made many raids across China's border. The Manchus had large, well-trained armies. Now, one of these armies was marching on Peking, the capital of the Chinese Empire.

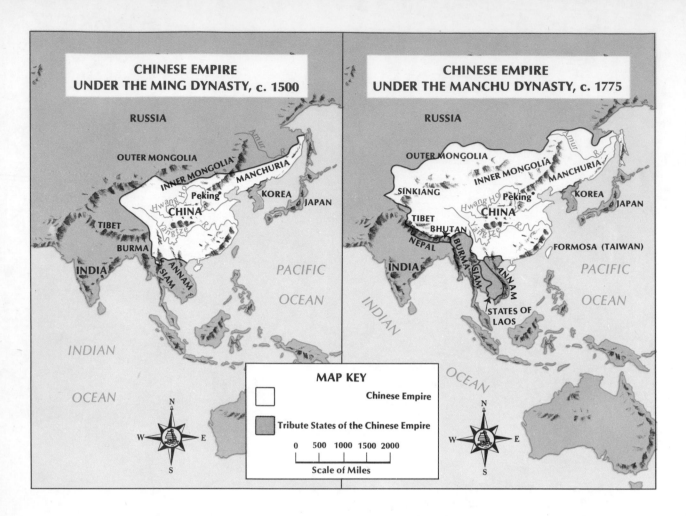

CHINESE EMPIRE
UNDER THE MING DYNASTY, c. 1500

CHINESE EMPIRE
UNDER THE MANCHU DYNASTY, c. 1775

MAP KEY

Chinese Empire

Tribute States of the Chinese Empire

0   500 1000 1500 2000
Scale of Miles

► Locate Manchuria on the maps above.

At the same time, an army of Chinese rebels was also marching on Peking. They wanted to overthrow the Ming emperor. The rebels reached Peking first. The emperor's generals were afraid the rebels would destroy the capital. Because they needed help, the generals turned to their Manchu enemies. The Manchus had not expected to be invited into China. They were happy to accept!

● Do you think the Chinese looked on the Manchus as barbarians? Why do you think they turned to them for help?

The Manchus defeated the rebels and drove them out of Peking. However, they refused to go home to Manchuria. They stayed on in China, took over the government, and founded a new dynasty.

► Why did the Manchus refuse to go home?

The Rise of the Manchu Dynasty

The Manchus called their dynasty Ch'ing (ching), which means "pure." However, we usually call it the **Manchu dynasty**. This dynasty lasted for nearly 300 years, until 1911.

The Manchus had easily taken control of China. Now they wanted to bring peace and prosperity back to the country. The Manchus were few in number compared to the millions of Chinese. Yet they were able to rule, and rule well, for many years. First, they brought order to the cities and provinces. Units of the Manchu army were set up throughout China. The soldiers helped keep the Chinese obedient to their Manchu rulers.

● Could the Manchus have ruled for 300 years through force alone? Explain.

The Manchus made the Chinese dress in a special way. Chinese men had to shave the front part of their heads and braid their hair in a long pigtail which hung down their backs. They had to wear tight sleeves that ended in a long, curved cuff. The cuff was shaped like a horse's hoof. This reminded the Chinese that they had been conquered by the nomadic horsemen of the steppes.

► What steppe people had conquered China before?

The Manchus did something more important, however. They won the loyalty of the Chinese by being wise and just rulers. The

Horse-hoof cuffs are an outstanding part of this gentleman's elegant clothing.

Manchus admired and respected Chinese civilization. In fact, they had adopted many Chinese ways when they lived on the steppe. The Manchus did not want to change or destroy Chinese civilization. They wanted to preserve the culture they admired so much. They honored the teachings of Confucius. They kept the Chinese system of government. They continued to appoint officials in the traditional way. This was through giving examinations in calligraphy (handwriting) and the Confucian Classics. As a result, many Chinese were given important positions in government.

● Were the Manchus wise to keep the traditional ways? What other conquerors of China had adopted Chinese customs?

★ Review some of Confucius' teachings about government.

Finally, the Manchu emperors started a program of territorial expansion. This means they expanded their control over more land. They wanted to make China safe from invasion.

First, the Manchus added their own homeland of Manchuria to the Chinese Empire. Manchuria was a valuable territory. It had many forests and rivers, as well as good farmland. Then the Manchus began to deal with the problem of the lands to the north and west. These lands were the greatest threat to China's security.

The Reign of K'ang Hsi

K'ang Hsi (käng' shē) was the first great Manchu ruler. He was strong, full of energy, and wise. Besides being a fine warrior and ruler, K'ang Hsi was a scholar and a writer. He tried to learn much about the art and the philosophy of his time. He suggested that a new dictionary be written. This book of more than 80,000 Chinese characters is still widely used today.

K'ang Hsi traveled all over the empire. He worked for the welfare of his subjects. He saw that roads were improved, to encourage trade. He began a program of public works, to give people jobs. He built irrigation systems, to improve farming. He also lowered taxes.

▶ What is meant by *public works*?

The varied education and many interests of K'ang Hsi resulted in a mixture of Chinese and Western ideas.

When he had improved conditions within China, K'ang Hsi turned his attention to protecting China's borders. He decided first to conquer Mongolia and make it part of the Chinese Empire. Mongolia lay on China's northern frontier. The Mongol nomads had given China trouble for many years.

The Mongol tribes were not united. Some tribes in Southern, or Inner, Mongolia were already under Manchu control. One of these tribes rebelled against the Manchus. This gave K'ang Hsi the chance to send his armies into Inner Mongolia to put down the rebellion. He then claimed *all* of Mongolia for China. But this claim was not made good. The tribes of Outer Mongolia remained independent of China for many more years.

▶ Look at the maps on page 12. Locate Inner Mongolia, Outer Mongolia, and Tibet.

Manchu conquest followed a certain plan. The Manchus did not rush troops to the border whenever the steppe people invaded. Instead, they sent armies into the homeland of these people. When the homelands were defeated, the lands were made part of China. To make the new lands truly Chinese, the emperor sent Chinese citizens to settle and colonize them. He also stationed Manchu army units there to keep order. K'ang Hsi and later Manchu rulers followed this plan with great success.

● What things can happen to native inhabitants when colonists arrive and settle?

● Discuss the meaning of *imperialism*. What form of imperialism was the Manchu rule? Explain.

The Conquest of Tibet

One western tribe in Outer Mongolia had grown very powerful. It had conquered most of its neighboring tribes. The Manchus were afraid that a new Mongol Empire might be on the rise. Also, these Mongols were gaining power in Tibet, the mountainous land to the north of India. K'ang Hsi realized that in order to control Outer Mongolia, he had to control Tibet. He soon found a chance to do this.

▶ Why would the Chinese fear the rise of Mongol power?

● Why did K'ang Hsi think that he had to control Tibet in order to control Outer Mongolia?

The Tibetans were Buddhists. The Mongols also were Buddhists. They had adopted the religion during the time of Kublai Khan. The Buddhist leader of Tibet was called the Dalai Lama (dä lī' lä' mə). A quarrel arose over the choice of the next Dalai Lama. The Mongols favored one man. So, K'ang Hsi came out in favor of someone else. Manchu armies entered Tibet, and K'ang Hsi's choice became the new Dalai Lama. K'ang Hsi appointed men from his own government to direct the Dalai Lama. He stationed Chinese troops in the country. Tibet had become part of the Chinese Empire. Yet China still did not have firm control over Outer Mongolia.

K'ang Hsi and the Jesuit Missionaries

Many Jesuit missionaries had come from France to China during the time of the Ming dynasty. Jesuit priests were from a Catholic religious order. They were interested in teaching the Chinese about Christianity. They also wanted to teach the newest learning in every field. In the early days of the Ch'ing dynasty, all foreigners had been made to leave the kingdom. The Jesuits also had been told to leave. Now K'ang Hsi allowed the Jesuits to return to China. He invited many to come to his court. He enjoyed talking with them and hearing about European civilization. He

This Jesuit priest is working in the Study Room of the Peking Observatory. He is dressed in the robes of a high-ranking member of the Chinese court.

admired their learning and, especially, their scientific knowledge. The Jesuit priests translated many European books into Chinese for the emperor. They also translated Chinese books into French. They wrote a history of China and sent letters back to France, telling of their experiences in K'ang Hsi's court. In this way, K'ang Hsi kept in touch with another great ruler of the time, Louis XIV. In this way, too, France came to admire Chinese culture.

Trouble at the Border

You can see from a map, or globe, that the countries of China and Russia are close to each other. As the Chinese Empire became bigger, the borders of the two countries came closer together. This led to disagreement about the boundaries between Russia and China. Russian Cossacks were setting up colonies and trading forts along the Manchurian border. They were fighting with local tribes and collecting tribute from them. These tribes turned to the Manchu emperor for help.

● Was Russia also imperialistic? Explain.

K'ang Hsi saw that a boundary must be drawn between Chinese and Russian territory. But how could he deal with the Russians? The Chinese could not speak their language and the Russians could not speak Chinese. The Jesuit priests solved the problem. The priests understood Chinese. Both the priests and the Russians spoke Latin. The Jesuits and the Chinese met with the Russians. They worked out a boundary that satisfied China. K'ang Hsi was grateful to the Jesuits. In return for their help, he allowed them to spread the teachings of Christianity among the Chinese people.

The Jesuits who had lived in China for a long time understood the Chinese practice of ancestor worship. They knew it was part of the teachings of Confucius. They allowed Chinese Christians to go on worshipping their ancestors. However, priests of other Catholic orders wanted to stop ancestor worship. They thought it went against the teachings of the church. They asked the pope to decide which group was right. The pope decided that ancestor worship should not be allowed.

K'ang Hsi was very angry. He felt the European pope had no right to make decisions about China. He was so angry that he closed the churches and exiled most of the priests.

● How did the Chinese respect for ancestors strengthen the Chinese government? (Hint: Think of the teachings of Confucius.)

The Reign of Ch'ien Lung

The second great Manchu emperor was K'ang Hsi's grandson, Ch'ien Lung (chē en' lúng). His rule began 60 years after K'ang Hsi's death.

Ch'ien Lung was finally able to control the western Mongols of Outer Mongolia. He chose a loyal chief and made him the leader of the western Mongols. When this leader rebelled, Ch'ien Lung's armies moved in. This ended the Mongol threat. Ch'ien Lung made sure the steppe people were never again powerful enough to sweep across Asia into China. The Mongols' land was added to the empire. It was called **Sinkiang** (shin' jyän'). Once again, Chinese citizens were moved from their homes to colonize the western lands. Manchu army units were stationed throughout the province. At this point, the Chinese Empire was the largest it had ever been. China's population was also the largest in its history.

Chinese Culture Under the Manchus

The Manchu dynasty was a time of stability. It did not cause cultural change in China. This was partly because the Manchus greatly respected traditional Chinese culture and wanted to preserve it. There were also political advantages in keeping to the old ways. It made it easier for the Manchus to win the loyalty and obedience of their Chinese subjects. It made it easier to unite China's large population under Manchu rule.

Under the Manchus, art and literature followed traditional forms. Artists painted in the style of earlier artists. Many scholarly books were written, but they were based on the classical works of the past. The Ch'ing emperors encouraged the artists and scholars in their work. The Manchu dynasty is most famous for its beautiful porcelain dishes and vases. The porcelain makers, too, used traditional patterns and colors. Very few new art forms developed during this time. Still, many beautiful works of art were produced. All were in great demand in Europe and America.

▶ Why do you think we call porcelain dishes ''china''?

● Under the Manchus, were the Chinese more interested in perfecting old techniques or in discovering new knowledge? Give reasons for your answers.

● Compare the Manchu Chinese attitudes about knowledge and art with those of the Renaissance Italians.

At times, several artists would work to make a single piece of Manchu porcelain. Each man worked on the part that needed his special skill.

Closing the Ring Around China

Besides the new territories that they had conquered and colonized, the Manchus added tribute states to the empire. These were states that bordered on China but did not belong to it. All of these states were greatly influenced by Chinese culture. They adapted many Chinese customs to their own way of life. These countries included Korea, Siam, Burma, Nepal, and Annam. The tribute states were actually protectorates of the Chinese Empire.

▶ On the map of the Chinese Empire in 1775 on page 12, locate the tribute states of the Manchu dynasty.

China was now in no danger of being invaded by land. To the east lay the ocean. To the north lay desert and steppe. To the west were the mountains of Tibet. And to the south were the tribute states of the empire. The Manchus had closed the ring around China.

● Look at the map of the Chinese Empire in 1500 on page 12. Then look at the map of the empire in 1775. Now explain what "closing the ring around China" means.

The Ceremony of the Kowtow

Tribute states had to accept the Chinese emperor as their ruler. They sent presents to the Chinese emperor as tribute. This showed they recognized the power and greatness of China. The ambassadors bringing this tribute also had to kowtow to the emperor.

The **kowtow** is a sign of loyalty and respect to the emperor. The Chinese had performed the ceremony of the kowtow for centuries. It went something like this:

People gathered and stood before the emperor. When the emperor was seated on his throne, an official called out: "Kneel down!" Everyone knelt. "Knock your heads to the ground!" Everyone touched his head to the ground three times. "Stand up!" Everyone stood up. This ceremony was repeated three times.

The Chinese saw nothing unusual in this custom. They believed that China was the greatest and most civilized nation on earth. They believed that China contained "all that was under Heaven." The kowtow simply meant accepting the authority of the emperor who ruled with the Will of Heaven.

● Do most people believe their culture is better than other cultures? Explain.

The Coming of the European Merchants

The Chinese had always believed that their culture was the best in the world. They had reason to be proud of it. Chinese civilization and culture had ancient origins and noble traditions. The Chinese did not seek contact with other cultures. They were not interested in foreign ideas or foreign goods. They had built a society on the foundations of their own past.

However, Europeans had been interested in China since the days of the Yuan dynasty and the travels of Marco Polo. They were curious about the Far East. They were also eager for trade. The British and Dutch tried to make trading agreements with the Manchu emperor. They were refused. The Chinese did not think of European nations as their equals either in power or in culture. They regarded them simply as barbarians.

The Manchus had made China safe from the danger of land invasion. But they had not considered another kind of invasion. That was invasion by the curious and restless Europeans crossing the ocean in their ships.

Europeans had been sailing to China ever since the sixteenth century. The early navigators and explorers were the first to come. They were followed by Christian missionaries. Then came merchants from Portugal, the Netherlands, and Great Britain.

The European merchants were eager for Chinese goods. They felt they had a right to trade. However, the Chinese were not interested in trading with the West.

Why didn't China want to trade with the West? One reason was that the Chinese distrusted foreigners. Another reason was that there was little demand for Western goods in China. The huge Chinese Empire and the nearby islands supplied almost everything that people needed. The only imports the Chinese

Chinese soldiers, holding banners which show the dragon symbol of the emperor, meet a ship arriving from Great Britain.

wanted were furs from the American Northwest, spices from the East Indies, and sandalwood from Hawaii. However, Chinese tea, porcelain, and silk were in great demand in the West. China held the upper hand in trade. So, it was able to limit the activity of the Western merchants.

Trading at Canton

European merchants were allowed to trade at only one port city. This was Canton (kan ton'), in southern China. They were not even allowed to enter the city! Warehouses, offices, and living quarters were built for them along the river banks. All trade was carried on with a special group of Chinese merchants. Europeans were not allowed to travel within the empire. They were not allowed to study or speak the Chinese language. If they complained about this treatment, the emperor simply stopped the trade.

During the early trading days, European countries sent ambassadors to the Manchu court. These ambassadors wanted their nations to have greater freedom to trade and to travel. They wanted their nations to be treated as China's equals. When they arrived at court, however, they were made to kowtow to the emperor. Their countries were not thought of as equal to China. Their gifts were received as tribute. They did not get the trading rights they wanted. It was very difficult for Europeans to deal with the Chinese. They did not like kowtowing to the emperor.

▶ Look up the word *ambassador*. What is the job of an ambassador?

▶ Why would the kowtow be a problem to Europeans?

▶ How were Western merchants treated? Would you say they were *segregated*? Explain.

● What would the Europeans think of their treatment by the Chinese?

In 1793, the British sent an ambassador to China. He was Lord Macartney. Lord Macartney was to ask the emperor for equal treatment for Westerners in China. He set out with a staff of 100 men. He also carried with him 600 cases of gifts and a letter from King George III to Emperor Ch'ien Lung.

▶ What have you learned about King George III?

When they reached the coast of China, the British were met by a fleet of royal barges. These barges had been sent by the emperor. As the ships traveled up the river to Peking, people crowded the banks to get a glimpse of the foreigners. Everywhere they stopped, the British were given parties and feasts.

At the court in Peking, Lord Macartney first presented the emperor with the gifts sent by King George. The emperor and his officials greatly admired these gifts. They especially liked one gift. This was a splendid coach with glass windows and velvet seats. However, they were shocked to see that the driver's seat was higher than the emperor's seat. This seemed a sign of disrespect to the Son of Heaven. So, the driver's seat was lowered.

After the gifts were accepted, Lord Macartney brought up the matter of the kowtow. He suggested that he show respect to the emperor in the same way he showed loyalty to his own king. This was by kneeling on one knee.

Ch'ien Lung and his court seemed pleased by this solution. Ch'ien Lung accepted the letter from King George. He then presented Lord Macartney with many gifts and a letter for the British king.

Then Lord Macartney and his men left for home. The British were sure their visit had been a success. They felt sure they had opened the door to friendship and equal trade with the Chinese. They were to be greatly disappointed. Ch'ien Lung's letter to King George was opened. This is part of what it said:

> You, O King, live in a distant region, far beyond the borders of many oceans, but desiring humbly to share the blessings of our civilization, you have sent an ambassador respectfully bearing your letter. . . . To show your devotion, you have also sent offerings of your country's products. I have read your letter: it shows a respectful humility on your part, which is highly praiseworthy. . . .
>
> As to your request to send an ambassador to be part of my Heavenly Court and to be in control of your country's trade with China, this request is contrary to all the ways of my dynasty and cannot possibly be granted. . . . How can our dynasty change its whole way of acting in order to do what you ask? . . .
>
> I have accepted your tribute offerings, O King, only because of the devotion which made you send them so far. Our dynasty's majestic virtue has reached every country under Heaven, and Kings of all nations have sent their costly tribute by land and sea. As your Ambassador can see for himself, we possess all things. I have no interest in strange and costly objects, and have no use for your country's products. . . .
>
> Up to now, all European merchants, including your own country's barbarian merchants, have carried on their trade with our Heavenly Empire at Canton. Such has been

the way for many years, although our Heavenly Empire possesses all things in great abundance and lacks no product within its own borders. There was therefore no need to import the manufactures of outside barbarians in exchange for our own produce. But as the tea, silk, and porcelain which the Heavenly Empire produces are necessary to Europeans, we have permitted, as a special favor, that a foreign trade center should be established at Canton, so that your wants might be supplied and your country thus participate in our kindness. But your Ambassador has now put forward new requests [for other trade bases] which completely fail to recognize the Throne's principle to "treat strangers from afar with kindness," and to have a peaceful control over barbarian

tribes, the world over. . . . It is best that the regulations now in force should continue unchanged. . . .

Ever since the beginning of history, sage Emperors and wise rulers have given China a moral system and code of behavior, which has been followed by the millions of my subjects. There is no desire for new and different teachings. . . . Your Ambassador's request that barbarians shall be given full freedom to preach their religion is utterly unreasonable.

It may be, O King, that these requests have been foolishly made by your Ambassador on his own, or perhaps you yourself did not know our ways when you expressed these wild ideas and hopes. . . . Your demands are contrary to the customs of our dynasty and would bring no good result. . . . I have commanded your tribute messengers to leave in peace on their homeward journey. It is your duty, O King, to respect our wishes and to display even greater devotion and loyalty in the future, so that by ever-continuing submission to our throne, you may secure peace and prosperity for your country hereafter. . . . Tremble and obey!

- What requests had the British made to the emperor? Had the emperor granted any of the requests?

- Discuss what the emperor's letter tells you about what the Chinese thought of themselves and their country. What did the Chinese think of foreigners?

- How did Ch'ien Lung's use of the word *barbarian* differ from the way we have been using this word in *The Human Adventure*?

- How would you describe Manchu imperialism? What examples can you find of *colonization, conquest and rule,* or *protectorates*? Are there examples of *economic imperialism* in the Manchu Empire?

- The chapter has given some interesting examples of *culture contact.* How would you describe the culture contact between the Manchu conquerors and the conquered Chinese? Was there *acculturation*? Which culture was stronger, the Chinese or the Manchurian?

chapter 2

Western Imperialism in China

Many Empires: Non-Western and Western

We have studied an example of non-Western imperialism—the Manchu Empire. There were other non-Western empires at about the same time. There was, for example, the Ottoman Empire that dominated Eastern Europe, North Africa, and part of the Middle East from the fourteenth to the eighteenth century. Another great Muslim Empire was the Mogul Empire in India. The Mogul conquerors ruled India from the sixteenth to the eighteenth century. There was the Russian Empire, too, which expanded into Siberia and Central Asia.

At the same time, Western empires were growing. Spain, Portugal, France, the Netherlands, and Britain all made conquests or set up colonies in different parts of the world.

Western imperialism usually developed in several stages. It developed for many different reasons. First, traders came for the goods and raw materials that were in demand in Europe. As trading posts were set up, soldiers were often needed to protect

Flags flying at the port of Canton showed which Western nations were permitted trade with China.

them. The traders and soldiers were later joined by Christian missionaries. These people wanted to spread the teachings of the church abroad. They also wanted to educate native people in Western ideas. In some lands, European colonies grew up. These colonies might include farmers and businessmen. All these people needed the protection of their government. They wanted to live under Western law and practice Western customs.

Western governments wanted to control these lands and their resources. Western industries needed raw materials. Western economies needed new markets. This led to struggles between European powers for empires. It also led to conflict between Western imperialist powers and the native countries.

We cannot try to study all these empires. Instead, we shall look more closely at three examples of Western imperialism. First, we shall look at the way in which Britain and other Western nations dominated China. Then we shall see how Britain built an empire in India. Lastly, we shall see how Britain and other Western nations took over parts of Africa.

- Review what you have learned about the controlling ideas of China and the West. How do you think their concepts of imperialism might differ?

▶ Review the different types of imperialism described in Chapter 1. As you read on, try to decide which type of imperialism is being studied.

The Chinese Trade

During the nineteenth century, Western Europeans continued to seek greater contact with China. The Chinese, however, continued to look on them as barbarians. European officials still had to kowtow to the Manchu emperor and pay him tribute. European traders were still limited to dockside warehouses in the port city of Canton.

- Review what you have learned about Chinese culture. Why did the Chinese look on all foreigners as barbarians? How had many Greeks looked on foreigners?

Workers in a Chinese "hong," or warehouse, busily weigh chests packed with tea. The owner uses an abacus to keep count of the shipment.

Although there were many difficulties, more and more Western traders came to Canton. They eagerly bought the Chinese goods that were in great demand in their countries—silk, porcelain, and tea. However, there was little demand for European products in China.

● From what you have learned, explain why there was little demand for European products in China.

Little demand for foreign products caused a serious economic problem. European merchants had to pay for Chinese goods with gold and silver **currency**. These cash payments led to a **gold outflow** from the treasuries of Europe. The European nations could not afford the constant drain of gold from their treasuries. They needed to find a product for which the Chinese would be willing to *trade*. Before long, they found such a product. It was **opium** (ō′ pē əm). The **opium trade** grew rapidly. It finally led to war between China and Great Britain.

● Why did the gold outflow have to stop? What happens to a nation's economy when it must pay cash for imported goods?

The Opium Market

Opium is a habit-forming drug. Small amounts of it are used in medicine. However, it damages the minds of those who use it steadily. It destroys their health. At first, opium smoking makes a person feel happy and strong. He comes to depend on it. After a time, his major interest is to get more opium. However, the drug is really poisoning him. The opium smoker becomes thin and sick and cannot think clearly. It is nearly impossible for him to stop using opium because he has become *addicted* to it. Many people who use opium frequently die from the poisoning.

★ Find out about other habit-forming drugs. What social problems do they cause?

The Opium Trade

The British, Dutch, Portuguese, and Americans all sold opium to the Chinese. The trade was illegal from the start. The emperor had forbidden the sale of opium in China. However, opium found a large market, especially in Chinese cities. China had

A visit to an opium den in Canton

many large and crowded cities. Many of the people who lived in them were very poor. They had miserable living conditions. They often did not have enough to eat. When there were crop failures, many people starved. So, some people were willing to buy opium when they could get it. Opium smoking made their lives seem less hopeless.

▶ Why would opium find a large market in China?

The British soon supplied almost all of the opium to China. Opium is made from poppies. Great Britain controlled India where many opium poppies were grown. British merchants brought chests of opium in cargo ships to islands off the coast of China. There, the Chinese merchants who cooperated in the trade bought their supplies. In turn, they sold the opium to the Chinese people. The opium trade made very large profits. It also solved the problem of the gold outflow from Europe to China.

Opium addiction became widespread throughout the Manchu Empire. In 1836, 26,000 chests of opium were smuggled into China. Each chest weighed 150 pounds. The emperor begged Queen Victoria to put an end to the trade for humanitarian reasons. **Humanitarianism** means a love for one's fellow men and a concern for their well-being. However, the British Parliament refused to end the trade. Opium had become too important as a source of wealth. The British did not want to give it up.

The Opium War

In 1839, two events brought matters to a head. First, the Chinese emperor had more than 20,000 chests of opium seized and burned in the harbor of Canton. He ended all trade with the West until the smuggling ended. The British were angered by the loss. However, because the sale of opium was illegal, they could not argue about it. Resentment and anger deepened on both sides.

The second event concerned the legal rights of foreigners in China. Some drunken British sailors killed a Chinese peasant. The Chinese demanded that the guilty man be turned over to them for punishment. The British refused. Chinese law was quite different from British law. Besides, the British did not know

Sea battle during the Opium War. Locate the British warship. Find the Chinese "warjunks."

which sailor had committed the murder. To the Chinese, this made no difference. Any one of the British sailors would do. Under Chinese law, each member of a group was responsible for the actions of the others.

The Chinese sent warships to seize the sailor. The British opened fire and sank four of the Chinese ships. This was the beginning of the **Opium War** between China and Great Britain. It was also the time when the culture of Western Europe came into open conflict with the culture of China.

Discuss these questions. You may get into arguments about some of them, just as the British and the Chinese did!

- Should all countries treat each other as equals?

- Should all countries trade with other countries freely? If a country does not want to trade with other countries freely, should it be forced to?

- Does a country have the right to make regulations on its trade with other countries? Can it make any regulations it wants?

- Did the Chinese emperor have the right to order that no more opium was to be imported into China? Did he have the right to seize and burn the opium of the British merchants?

- Should the British government have made British merchants stop carrying opium to China? Why do you suppose it did not?

- If a person commits a crime in a foreign country, should he be punished by his own country, or by the country where he committed the crime?

The Opium War lasted for three years. The Manchu emperors had a long history of victory over barbarians. As we have seen, they looked on the British as barbarians from across the sea. However, Manchu forces were no match for British naval power. The British fleet, armed with cannon, attacked Chinese port cities in the south. They easily defeated the Chinese, who were armed with bows, spears, and old-fashioned firearms.

The "Unequal Treaties"

When the war ended, the British drew up the peace terms, or **treaty**. This treaty came to be known as an "unequal treaty." It was the first of many "unequal treaties" between China and the West.

- What do you think an unequal treaty is?

The British terms were very harsh. The British wanted to open all of China to free trade. So, five Chinese cities, including Canton and Shanghai (shang' hī'), were declared **open ports**. Foreigners would be allowed to live in these cities. The Chinese government was to receive British ambassadors as equals. The island of Hong Kong, off the south coast of China, was given to Great Britain. In addition, the Chinese were made to pay the costs of the war. The Chinese also had to pay the value of the opium they had destroyed. This came to 21 million dollars.

The treaty, however, did not decide the question whether foreigners who were guilty of crimes would be tried under Chinese law.

The Chinese defeat was complete. The Chinese had been greatly humbled by the British. The smuggling of opium continued on an even larger scale.

► How did Western technology help to weaken China? (Think of Western weapons and sea power.)

● Why were the Western nations able to force China into unequal treaties?

● Do you think unequal treaties are wise? Why or why not?

● How do you think the Chinese looked on Westerners after their defeat? Would they respect them, or hate them, or both?

Other Western nations demanded the same privileges that Great Britain had won as a result of the war. The United States had entered the Canton trade shortly after the Revolutionary War. Soon, France, Russia, and the United States all signed new treaties with China. These countries did not want Britain to control all the trade with China. None of them wanted the British to become more powerful than itself.

British merchants sold products from England and her colonies to the Chinese.

The treaty between China and the United States settled the problem of whether a foreign citizen was subject to Chinese law. It stated that Americans who committed crimes in China were to be tried in American courts under American law. Other nations gained the same legal rights for their citizens.

In each of the open Chinese ports, foreigners lived together in separate communities called *settlements*. All of them lived under the laws of their own countries. These foreign settlements became independent colonies in the heart of some of China's largest cities.

- How do you imagine the Chinese felt about these settlements?

The opium trade was made legal. However, the Chinese emperor and government never took part in it. The Chinese, except for a few dishonest merchants and officials, made no profit from it. The Chinese stated their feeling toward the British this way: "China sends tea to England to make you into gentlemen; England sends opium to China to make us into slaves."*

▶ What did the Chinese mean by this statement?

The conflict between China and the West grew more and more serious. The Chinese hated the Westerners and tried to keep them out of their cities. Sometimes foreigners who stepped outside their settlements were murdered.

This hatred and distrust led to another war in 1858. Once again, the Chinese were defeated. Once again, an unequal treaty was made. Europeans won additional rights and territory. Foreign ambassadors were allowed to live in the royal city of Peking.

Foreigners began to travel freely throughout China. Christian missionaries once again preached their faith to the Chinese. Western ideas began to come into China. Western influence grew greatly. As it did, Chinese resentment grew stronger.

▶ What had happened to Christian missionaries under the rule of K'ang Hsi?

*Dennis Bloodworth, *The Chinese Looking Glass* (New York: Farrar, Straus & Giroux, Inc., 1966), pp. 357–58.

Rebellion in China

During the time Europeans were growing stronger in China, the Manchu dynasty had been growing weak. The Manchus had lost to the Europeans in war. They had lost control of trade. They had lost the right to administer Chinese justice to foreigners. During the 1860's, the Manchus lost control of their own subjects, too. Terrible riots and rebellion broke out all over the country.

Many Chinese wanted major changes. They wanted more land and lower taxes for the peasants. Many Chinese wanted to adopt some Western ideas, especially in trade and technology. They thought this would help them to control the foreigners. Others wanted to drive out the foreigners altogether. Still others wanted to overthrow the Manchu dynasty, which they considered just as foreign as the Europeans.

▶ Why did some Chinese consider the Manchus foreign? From where had the Manchus come?

● Do you think that all these different views could be united easily?

From Trade to Imperial Power

The Western powers had always considered China a mighty empire. They were surprised at how easily they had defeated China. The Western nations had gained all the rights they wanted. Now they wanted other things from China. China was rich in fertile farmland and valuable minerals. The Europeans wanted to control and develop these resources. However, several powerful nations were competing for this control. Great Britain, Russia, France, and Germany all wanted pieces of China. These countries watched one another jealously. None wanted any of the others to become more powerful than itself.

● Was this a help to China? Would China have been better off if only *one* foreign country had been interested in conquest?

The Europeans began their expansion by taking over many of China's tribute states. These states became the base for European imperial power in the East.

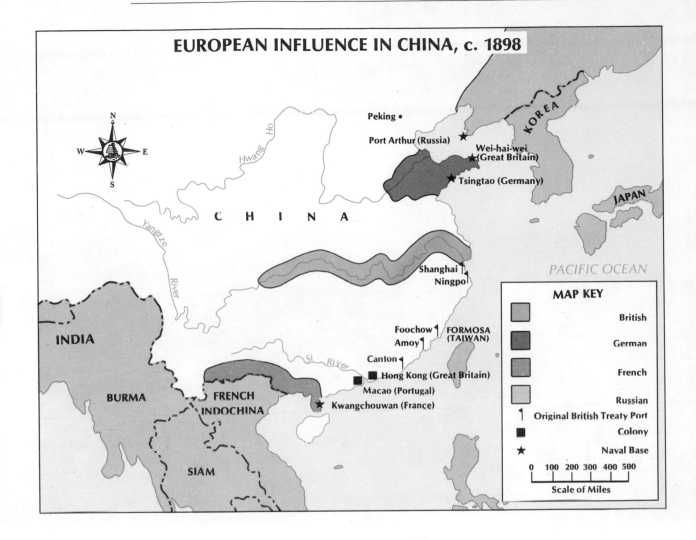

EUROPEAN INFLUENCE IN CHINA, c. 1898

Peking •

Port Arthur (Russia) ★

Wei-hai-wei (Great Britain) ★

Tsingtao (Germany) ★

KOREA

JAPAN

C H I N A

Hwang Ho

Yangtze River

Shanghai

Ningpo

PACIFIC OCEAN

Foochow

Amoy

FORMOSA (TAIWAN)

Canton

Si River

Hong Kong (Great Britain)

Macao (Portugal)

Kwangchouwan (France) ★

INDIA

BURMA

FRENCH INDOCHINA

SIAM

MAP KEY

British

German

French

Russian

Original British Treaty Port

Colony

Naval Base

0 100 200 300 400 500

Scale of Miles

▶ Look at the map above. Notice the European expansion. Compare it with the map of the Chinese Empire under Manchu power on page 12.

In the Chinese Empire, the European nations did not conquer and rule. Instead, they divided the empire into spheres of influence. A **sphere of influence** is an area where one particular nation has special rights and power. Thus Russia controlled trade in northeast China. Britain controlled trade around Shanghai and on the Yangtze River. France and Germany, too, had spheres of influence. Japan, however, actually went to war with China, and conquered Korea and Formosa. (Formosa is now called Taiwan.)

The port city of Canton was affected by the decline of the Manchu reign. During the conflicts for foreign influence in China, the factories and much of the city were destroyed in war.

● Why was China so helpless in the face of foreign interference?

● How would you describe Western imperialism and Japanese imperialism in China?

★ Who rules Korea and Taiwan today? When and how did Japan lose these lands?

The United States had no sphere of influence in China. At the end of the nineteenth century, it was still busy developing its own territory. In 1901, the United States asked for an **Open Door** policy in China. The purpose of the Open Door policy was to prevent the division of China into spheres of influence. It came too late.

The Impact of the West

China had been invaded by barbarians many times during its long history. Each time, it had preserved its civilization from invaders. However, the Europeans were a different kind of invader. They came from a culture that was as strong as the culture of China. Their culture was still young and growing. People in Europe were restless. They loved to experiment with new ways of thinking and doing. Chinese culture, on the other hand, was much older. It was traditional and stable.

The restless and curious Europeans had developed high technologies and trading economies. Through trade and exploration, they had expanded into other parts of the world. Their activities finally led them to imperialism. Europeans wanted to extend their control over other lands and peoples.

Under the Manchus, the Chinese, too, had been imperialistic. However, their purpose had been to make the borders of their empire safe from invasion. They wanted to protect China from contact with the outside world.

In many ways, contact with the West proved very harmful for China. Still, it brought many important changes very quickly. Western scholars came to China. Chinese scholars traveled to Western Europe and the United States. The Chinese lost confidence in their Manchu rulers. The Manchu dynasty grew weaker and weaker. It was finally overthrown in 1911. The Manchu was the last Chinese dynasty. It was followed by a republican government. An exchange of ideas began between East and West. This exchange included ideas about government, religion, philosophy, art, and technology.

- What political ideas do you think China got from the West?

- What ideas do you think the West got from China?

★ What kind of government does China have today? (Remember, there are two Chinas.)

chapter 3

Western Imperialism in India

Western imperialism in China was mainly *economic imperialism*. It was, however, backed by military force. Let us look at another type of Western imperialism, this time in India.

The Mogul Empire

Europeans came to India in the last years of the **Mogul Empire**. The Moguls were Muslim Turks who had conquered India during the sixteenth century. They united almost all of the subcontinent under their rule. The Moguls founded a Muslim dynasty that lasted for about 300 years.

However, most of the people they ruled were not Muslims. They were Hindus. The beliefs of the Hindus were very different from those of their Muslim rulers.

● What were the controlling ideas of Islam, the Muslim religion? (Think especially of the idea of "holy war.") Can you see how some Islamic ideas would lead to conflict with other cultures?

During the Mogul Empire, a small number of Muslims governed millions of Hindus. Sometimes they ruled with wisdom. At

European influence in India is reflected in this picture of an Indian emperor at his court. King James I of England appears at the bottom.

Muslims were forbidden to represent any living thing. Instead, they used designs and their alphabet in their art. Hindu artists believed that their purpose was to show many forms of God. Mogul art combined Muslim and Hindu ideas.

other times, however, the Mogul emperors were cruel and unjust. They tried to force Hindus to become Muslims. They destroyed Hindu temples and statues. They tried to break down the Hindu way of life.

Still, some parts of Hindu Indian culture mixed with some parts of Islamic culture. From this mixing, a rich new culture developed. Splendid buildings were put up. Beautiful works of art were produced.

Finally, however, the Mogul Empire began to fall apart. The last great Mogul emperor died in 1707. The age of Islamic expansion was over. For the next 150 years, India was in a state of unrest. Hindus and Muslims fought each other. Peasant rebellions broke out all over the empire. Strong central government ended.

In the midst of this confusion, Western Europeans arrived in India.

Early Trade with India

The Portuguese were the first Europeans to come to India. During the sixteenth century, they won trading rights from the Mogul Empire. They set up trading posts around Goa on India's west coast. Locate Goa on a map of the world. The king of Portugal called himself "Lord of the Seas." He tried to prevent other countries from trading in India.

The Portuguese were interested in more than trade. They wanted to establish their power in India. They also wanted to send Christian missionaries to teach and convert the Indian people.

However, the Portuguese had powerful rivals in the Arab traders. The Christian Portuguese hated the Muslim Arabs. The Portuguese defended their trading posts with soldiers and cannon. They drove the Arab ships out of the harbor. They also supported Hindus against Muslims in local quarrels.

► What Portuguese seaman had sailed to India in the late fifteenth century?

★ When did Portugal lose control of Goa?

The scenes on this cotton bedspread show Portuguese merchants in the palace of a 17th-century Indian nobleman. They are probably discussing trading privileges.

- Why would the Christian Portuguese hate the Arab Muslims? (Clue: What people conquered much of Spain and Portugal in the Middle Ages?)

Early in the seventeenth century, other European nations sent traders to India. The English, Dutch, and French were also eager to trade for the goods of the Indies.

▶ What goods from the Indies were in demand in Western Europe?

The Dutch and the English struggled for control of the Spice Islands. The Dutch won control. The English traders were driven back to the mainland of India.

- Locate the Spice Islands on a map in your classroom. Why were they important to trade? What are the Spice Islands called today?

The East India Company

English trade was carried on by a group called the East India Company. It had been chartered by Queen Elizabeth in 1600. The company was a private group of merchants. They had been granted the right to conduct all British trade in the East Indies.

In the seventeenth century, the East India Company won trading rights from the Mogul emperor. But during this period, the Mogul government was in decline. The country became weak and divided. Groups of warlike Hindus were rising up against their Muslim rulers. There was constant danger of invasion across the northern borders. Large parts of India were ruled by local princes. These princes were not always able to maintain law and order. They were not always able to protect their people.

The English established trading posts along the east coast of India. As the Portuguese had done, the English **fortified**, or defended, these posts with soldiers and cannon. This made them safe from raids and attacks. The trading forts protected the surrounding area. As these areas were made safe, Indians came to settle nearby. As time passed, cities began to grow up around the early trading forts. Two of these cities are Madras (ma dräs') and Calcutta (kal kut'ə). Find these cities on a map of the world.

Europeans imported many items from India. Among them were this water pipe, bronze spice pot, feathered fan, and inlaid box all displayed on this colorful cotton shawl, itself a much desired Indian product. Below, is an Indian chess set. The board is of inlaid marble and the chessmen are carved of ivory. Europeans found it interesting that the pieces represented figures from Indian culture rather than the knights and bishops which were more familiar to Western culture.

The Growth of Trade

The English had not been in India long when they found they had a serious trading problem. Indian spices, jewels, and works of art were in great demand in England. However, England's major product, manufactured woolen goods, was in no demand at all in India. The East India Company was unable to *trade* with the Indian merchants. The English were forced to pay for Indian goods with gold and silver currency. However, the English government did not want to pay out currency for Indian goods.

● Why not? What would happen to a nation's economy if all imported goods had to be paid for with gold?

● Where else did this problem arise? What was the solution?

The East India Company found an answer to this problem. It developed a trade by becoming partners with some of the Indian merchants and craftsmen. Indian craftsmen wove a soft cotton cloth in beautiful designs. This cloth was in demand both in England and elsewhere in the East. The East India Company sold the cloth that the Indians produced. The English ships could carry large cargos. They delivered Indian cloth to other Eastern ports. In return, they got silks, porcelains, and spices. The English also made enough money profit to pay for Indian goods. When the cloth began to be manufactured on a large scale, it could be sold cheaply. This early partnership grew into an important industry in India.

British Political Influence in India

Through this early trade, the East India Company began to have great influence in India. Its operations grew larger and larger. Many Englishmen came to India as employees of the trading company. Meanwhile, the decline of Mogul power had ended central government in India.

The merchants were no longer dealing with an emperor. Instead, they had to deal with local princes who ruled the provinces. These princes were often involved in wars with each other. To protect its trade, the East India Company often had to take sides with one prince or another. In this way, the British were drawn into local wars and struggles for power.

In return for British support, some of the princes granted territory to the East India Company. The company began to rule these territories. It appointed British officials to run them. The company also put together an army to protect these territories.

The British began to introduce their own institutions to India. The company ran its territory according to English law. British authority was backed up by well-trained armies. The armies were made up of British and Indian soldiers. The local princes still ruled in their provinces. However, their power depended on British support.

Even though the East India Company was gaining political power in India, it did not represent the British government. It acted simply for itself. In the beginning, the company was not interested in conquest, or missionary work, or the struggle for power in India. It was interested only in trade. But the importance of trade made it deeply involved in Indian political life.

● We have seen how *economic* imperialism was leading to another type of imperialism. What is this other type?

The Seven Years' War

The British were not the only Europeans active in the Indies trade. The Portuguese still controlled the area around Goa, on the west coast. The Dutch controlled the Spice Islands. However, the greatest threat to British trade in India came from France. The power struggle between the British and French traders came to a head in 1740. Both nations sent armed forces to India. The battle for control of the India trade was part of the **Seven Years' War**, a conflict that was fought in many parts of the world.

★ Find out about the Seven Years' War Where was it fought outside of India? Which battles were fought in North America? What do we call the part that was fought in North America? Which battles were fought in Europe?

The war in India seesawed back and forth between the French and the British. The French won several important land

Robert Clive led the British to victory at Plassey. French and Indian troops were defeated, and British rule in eastern India was firmly established.

battles. However, their victories were offset by British naval power. The British fleet was able to cut off supplies to the French land forces. The British finally won the war.

★ Find out about the Battle of Plassey (plä′ sē), and Robert Clive, leader of the British forces.

The struggle in India between France and Great Britain began as a struggle for control of trade. It then turned into a struggle for political control. The struggle became imperialistic. Both nations wanted to control the vast resources of India. Neither wanted its trade routes cut off by the other. Both France and Great Britain were rich, proud, and powerful nations. Both were eager to extend their political and economic control to other parts of the world. Still, even after the war, the British government did not control India directly. It left control in the hands of the East India Company.

At this point, we should ask ourselves why the British were able to move in so quickly to take control of India. There are several important reasons.

When the Mogul dynasty lost power, there was a fierce power struggle among many warring Indian groups. India was weak and divided. It was a little like Western Europe during the age of feudalism. No one group was strong enough to unite the subcontinent. Only the British were strong enough to step in and bring order to India.

Another reason was the religion of most of the people in India. This was **Hinduism**. Hinduism is both a religion and a way of life. All Hindus lived in a **caste system**. It was like the caste system that Buddha found when he was growing up in India more than two thousand years earlier.

● How did Buddha feel about the caste system?

A girl of the Brahman caste   *A boy who is an outcaste*

Hindus were born into a caste and stayed in it all their lives. Their most important duties were the caste duties they carried out. Hindus in one caste did not think of Hindus in another caste as their equals. It was hard for Hindus to unite with each other. It was still harder for them to unite with Muslims. This was a major reason why the feeling of nationalism did not grow in India. It did not come until the twentieth century.

● Can you see why Hindu ideas might not fit in with the idea of nationalism? Explain.

By 1772, the East India Company dominated India. Its influence extended throughout the subcontinent. Many English traders made great fortunes in India. Other Englishmen became famous as governors and soldiers.

★ Find out about Warren Hastings, Lord Cornwallis, and Lord Wellesley. These men were early governors-general in India.

India Under British Rule

The British brought many improvements to India. They built up a strong government. They helped build up a strong and fair system of law. They helped to advance education and medical care. They built cities, roads, and irrigation systems. They improved the communication systems throughout India. They tried to end famine. They drove out invaders and brought peace to the country. They unified India under a single rule—British rule.

Still, as time passed, many British officials seemed to lose interest in the traditional Indian culture. Tradition was a powerful force in India. Many Hindu customs were holy. The Indian people did not always like or agree with European ideas and changes. They were afraid their own culture would be swept aside by these ideas. In some parts of India, resentment against the British had been growing quietly for many years. Many Indian landowners had lost their property to the British. A few British officials controlled millions of Indians. Indians had very little voice in their government. They had no way of making their wishes known. Some British soldiers and officials looked down on Indians and

A hotel in India during the time of British rule. Notice the expressions on the faces of the people. What ideas about the feelings between the British and Indian peoples does this picture give you?

treated them harshly. They forgot that their first dealings with the Indians had been as *partners*. In 1857, Indian feeling against the British exploded. That was the year of the **Indian Mutiny**, or **Sepoy** (sē′ poi) **Rebellion**.

The Indian Mutiny

The **sepoys** were Indian soldiers who were trained and equipped by the East India Company. They were excellent soldiers. They fought alongside British soldiers in regiments, or army units, commanded by British officers. These regiments were often hired by Indian princes to put down rebellions or drive out enemies. The British depended on the loyalty of the sepoys. The sepoys outnumbered the British soldiers seven to one. Some of the sepoys were Hindus. Some were Muslims.

Mutinous sepoys are surprised by British soldiers as they divide the spoils of their rebellion.

The ammunition used by the soldiers came in cartridges with greased ends. The soldier had to bite off the greased end to release the gunpowder before he could load his gun. Rumors began to spread through the army. Hindu soldiers were told that the cartridges were greased with beef fat. Cattle are sacred to the Hindus and may not be killed or eaten. Muslim soldiers were told that the cartridges were greased with pork fat. Muslims are forbidden to touch pork.

Both groups were extremely angry with the British. Indian soldiers turned on their British officers and murdered many of them. The British were shocked and frightened. With the help of Indians who were loyal to them, they finally ended the mutiny. The Sepoy Rebellion lasted for two years. It cost many lives and caused great suffering on both sides.

India Becomes Part of the British Empire

At this point, the British government stepped in. The East India Company was blamed for the rebellion. Parliament decided to rule India itself. In 1858, India became part of the British Empire. Queen Victoria later became the "Empress of India."

The British did not rule *all* of India directly. The subcontinent was divided into "British India" and native states. However, most of the native states came under the *indirect rule* of Great Britain. France and Portugal continued to rule small colonies in India also.

● How would you describe British imperialism in India? Colonization? Conquer and rule? Protectorate?

At this ceremonial gathering in Delhi in 1877, Queen Victoria is being proclaimed "Empress of India."

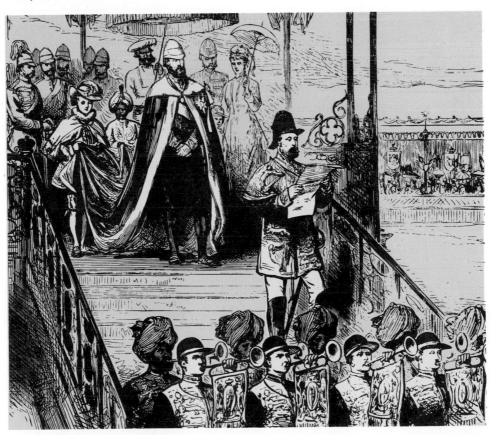

After the disaster of the Sepoy Rebellion, the British realized that Indians must be given a greater voice in their government. They established a *civil service*. Through the civil service, educated Indians could rise to high government positions. Many Indians began to study English in order to qualify for these posts. As Indians learned Western ideas and began to take part in government, the feeling of nationalism began to grow. A class of Indian lawyers, teachers, and writers came into being. Western ideas and Western technology took root. In addition, Indians wanted to copy British parliamentary government. For the first time, Indians thought in terms of the government's duties *to the people*. Indians began to think of themselves as a single nation. As the power of the local princes faded, the ideals of national pride and patriotism grew stronger. The growth of nationalism gave rise to a powerful movement for India's independence from Britain.

▶ How would education and improved communications help to spread the ideas of nationalism?

In 1885, the *Indian National Congress* was founded. Its goal was India's future independence. It wanted Indians to be given more power in government. The *Congress Party*, as it came to be called, was made up mainly of Hindus.

In general, Hindus were willing to learn the English language and English ways. They saw this as their opportunity to become self-ruling someday. However, Indian Muslims had their own history of imperial rule. They were not at home with Western traditions. They found it hard to join with the Hindus, who had been their subjects during the Mogul dynasty. The Muslims felt they had little chance of having a voice in an Indian government dominated by the Hindus and the British. Muslim and Hindu political interests began to grow apart. The Muslims formed their own political party—the *Muslim League*. The League worked for Muslim rights and representation in government.

As time passed, the British shared more and more power with the Indians. Still, the British made the final decisions. They controlled spending, foreign relations, and defense. Also, most

Indians were not allowed to vote because they did not own property. Poverty, illiteracy, famine, and disease were still widespread.

Discontent with British rule grew stronger. It led to an organized drive for Indian independence. In the twentieth century, this drive produced a remarkable Indian leader—Mahatma Gandhi (mə hät'mə gän'dē).

★ Find out about Gandhi and Nehru (nā' rü), leaders of the independence movement.

The subcontinent of India was granted independence in 1947. Two nations came into being, India, mostly Hindu, and Pakistan, mostly Muslim. A long chapter of Western imperialism was closed.

Indian nationalist leader and social reformer, Mahatma Gandhi (center), meets with members of the Congress Party.

chapter 4

Western Imperialism in Africa

India was not the only area affected by Western imperialism. Western Europeans also expanded into Africa. At first, Africa was important to Europeans only because it was on the route to India. As time passed, however, Africa itself became important. We shall see how Western contact with Africa led first to the slave trade, and then to imperial rule that lasted well into the twentieth century.

First, let us look at Africa's geography and history.

Natural Environment of Africa

The natural environment of Africa has played an important part in its history. It has had a great influence on the lives of African people.

A tribal mask showing the interaction of Western and African cultures

Africa has many kinds of landforms. Mountains, rivers, and deserts form natural boundaries. These boundaries separate one region from another. Africa has few good harbors. Although it has many long rivers, they are hard to navigate. Rapids and waterfalls block travel at many points. Tropical rain forests make it difficult to travel very far inland.

▶ Look at a physical map of Africa. Locate some of Africa's major landforms. Explain how they form boundaries between different regions.

● How would these boundaries affect the Africans' contact with one another? How would they affect African contacts with the outside world?

Africans have had to adjust their lives to their natural environment. Different environments produced different ways of life. Society, government, religion, economy, and art changed from one region in Africa to another. Many different cultures existed, but they were unknown to the rest of the world. Most of these cultures left no written records of their past.

Africans often moved from place to place. Sometimes they moved to escape from enemies or from a powerful ruler. More often, they moved to find better farming or pasture land. This, too, affected the growth of civilization in Africa.

● Why? What are the conditions for the growth of civilization?

Still, great civilizations did develop in Africa. In some areas, powerful kingdoms and wealthy trading centers developed. Some parts of Africa had a long history of trade with the Islamic world. They showed strong Muslim influence. North Africa had had contacts with Europe since the days of the Roman Empire. However, in some parts of Africa, civilization developed slowly, or not at all.

▶ Name an ancient African civilization.

● Review what you know about medieval African kingdoms. What was the basis of their power? How were they influenced by the outside world?

*The varied landforms of Africa include
deserts and lush rain forests,
dense jungles and vast grasslands,
great mountains and deep valleys.*

For centuries, Europeans had little knowledge of Africa. It was dangerous to sail too close to the shores of West Africa. Good harbors were few and far between. For a time, these fears kept Europeans from seeking contact with Africa.

▶ Why do you think Europeans called Africa the "Dark Continent"?

East Coast Cities

When Vasco da Gama sailed around Africa in 1497, he saw prosperous trading cities along Africa's east coast. These cities were the centers of the Indian Ocean trade, a trade controlled by Muslim Arabs. The Arabs had been trading with the East for many years. Arab ships brought goods from the East into the African ports. These goods included silks and porcelains from China, spices from India, and pearls from Arabia. In exchange, the ships took gold and ivory and some slaves from the interior of Africa.

As a result of trade, the east coast cities became wealthy and important. The Portuguese sailors were surprised to find beautiful and prosperous cities in Africa. They saw tall houses, painted white, set along the shores of the brilliant blue sea. They saw bustling marketplaces and harbors crowded with foreign ships. They also found that these rich trading centers were controlled by Muslims. The people in East Africa were greatly influenced by Islam. They had adopted some Islamic ideas and customs into their own culture. Many of them wore Islamic dress and practiced the Muslim religion.

► Which other African people had been influenced by Islam?

The Portuguese first came to Africa as traders, not conquerors. When the Africans pictured them, however, the Portuguese appeared dominant and overbearing, as in this 17th-century bronze statue.

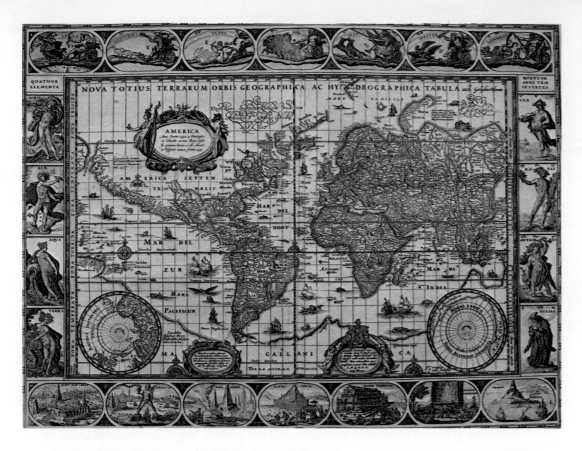

Continued exploration of Africa's coast allowed Europeans to make more accurate maps. Yet, this 16th-century map shows that there were still unknown areas of the world.

● Can you explain why Arabs were able to control the trade route between Africa and the Orient?

● How did Christian Portuguese feel about Muslim Arabs? Why?

The Portuguese sailors robbed and burned the East African cities. They left most of them in ruins. They sank Arab ships and occupied the eastern ports themselves. When the cities were destroyed, the Indian Ocean trade ended. Portugal did not have enough men, money, or ships to bring the trade back.

Soon, other Europeans followed the Portuguese to Africa. By the middle of the sixteenth century, Western Europe was trading with West Africa. Trading posts were set up along the coast, and trade agreements were made with local rulers. Europeans exchanged guns, cloth, and liquor for African pepper, gold, ivory, and vegetable oils. The West African states grew powerful on this trade. With the help of European firearms, these states were able to bring other African lands under their control.

A system of forced labor was a feature of colonial life in the New World empires of Spain and Portugal. This detail from a mural by Diego Rivera shows Indians being branded (center) and erecting Spanish palaces (top).

★ Find out about the rise of the *Ashanti Kingdom* during this period.

For a time, Africans and Europeans traded goods peacefully. Europeans and Africans treated each other with respect. Then, European nations began to develop their colonies in North and South America. This brought about a great change in their trade with Africa.

Beginning of the Atlantic Slave Trade

A large labor supply was needed to farm the land and mine the minerals of the New World. When Europeans first began to colonize the Americas, native American Indians did most of the work of clearing and farming the land. However, the Indians were not well suited to large-scale land cultivation. First, there were not enough of them to do the work. Second, many of them were not used to an organized system of labor. Third, many died from diseases that came from Europe.

Native Africans, on the other hand, were used to a system of labor. They were skillful farmers, miners, and metal workers. They were able to resist most diseases. Europeans decided to use Africans as workers in their American colonies.

● Which European nations had colonies in North and South America? Where were these colonies?

▶ Look at a map of the world. What parts of the Americas are in the same latitude as tropical Africa? Why would Africans be useful in these regions?

There was another important reason why Europeans turned to Africa as a source of laborers. Slavery was an old institution in Africa. For centuries, African rulers had made slaves of criminals and war captives. Some slaves were well treated. A few rose to important positions. Others worked in fields or mines. After the rise of Islam, Arab slave traders bought slaves in the heart of Africa and exported them to the Middle East and North Africa. In this way the slave trade became a big business.

It became much bigger with the coming of European slave traders. It took a different form, too. Its aim was different, as well. The Atlantic slave trade's aim was to supply slaves for the cash-crop plantations of the New World.

★ Find out more about slavery in different cultures. For example: in classical Greece and Rome, in the Islamic Empires, in West and East Africa, in medieval Europe, and in Russia.

The Spread of the Slave Trade

African chiefs who received firearms from the Europeans had a great advantage over Africans who had only metal spears and swords.

● Why were firearms an advantage? What had happened when firearms were introduced in the medieval African kingdoms?

Many of these African chiefs took part in the slave trade. They attacked weaker tribes. Then they rounded up the captured people and turned them over to the European traders.

In return for the captives, the chiefs received brandy, cloth, and more guns. With the help of some powerful African chiefs, the slave trade grew rapidly.

Why did some African chiefs take part in the slave trade? One reason was that they needed to defend their own people. They wanted to keep their own people from being taken as slaves. Another reason is that they extended their power over the lands they conquered.

- Do you think the slave trade could have succeeded without the help of these chiefs?

The captives were marched many miles from inland Africa to the coast. They were often loaded with valuable goods such as gold and ivory. Many Africans died along the way. Those who

Using every available inch of space, the captain of this ship, the Brookes was able to fit over 400 prisoners aboard. This was done with an eye to profit for the captain and no concern for the comfort of the Africans.

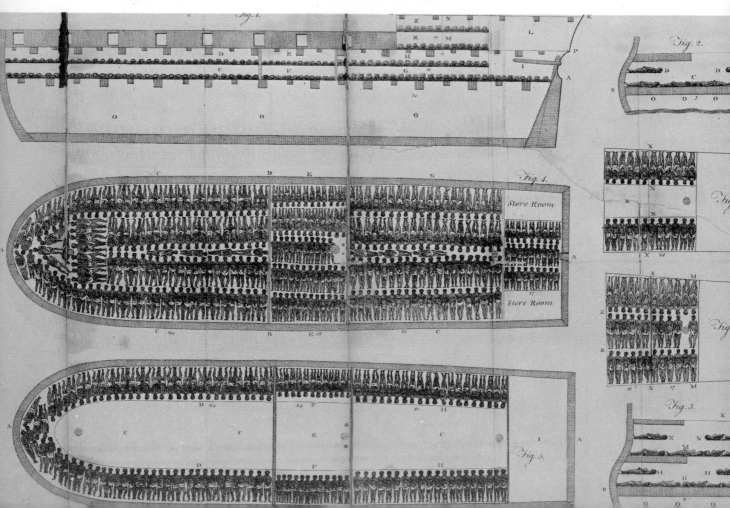

survived were delivered to the European traders at coastal forts. There they were divided into groups according to their age and sex. They were branded to show that they were slaves. Then they were loaded onto ships for the long voyage to the New World.

Historians have said that at least 15 million Africans made this journey between the seventeenth and nineteenth centuries. Many others died along the way.

Africans were stacked in the holds of the slave ships like "rows of books on shelves." They were chained together two by two. Each slave had his hands and legs tied. The ocean voyage took from six to ten weeks. Many Africans died from disease, rotting food, and the filthy conditions aboard ship. Some were killed. Some killed themselves. Sharks fed on the bodies of the dead which were thrown overboard.

At the end of the 18th century, Britain passed several humanitarian anti-slave trade laws. Britain tried to enforce these laws by the use of naval patrols. These slaves were rescued by the British from a ship such as the Brookes.

Still, enough Africans survived the trip to make the slave trade profitable. By the eighteenth century, the Great Triangular Trade Route was established. European traders brought manufactured goods to Africa. Here the goods were exchanged for slaves. The slaves were shipped to the Americas where they were sold to plantation owners. The shipowners were paid in sugar and tobacco. These goods were shipped back to Europe where they brought high prices.

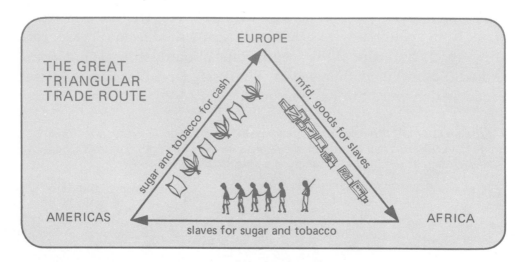

Many Europeans and Americans made great fortunes from the slave trade. Factory owners made large profits from the inexpensive manufactured goods they sent to Africa. Shipowners made a triple profit, first from exchanging cheap goods for slaves, next from selling slaves in the New World, then by selling American sugar and tobacco in Europe.

Europeans began to realize that Africa was very important to their economies. It was important mainly because it was the source of slaves. For Africa, however, the slave trade was harmful. It brought wars and suffering as the hunt for slaves increased. It robbed Africa of some of its youngest and strongest people. These people were usually chosen to become slaves in the New World. The slave trade slowed down the growth of civilization in some parts of Africa.

● How might slavery in the New World affect future relations between blacks and whites? Explain.

By the early seventeenth century, Great Britain, France, and the Netherlands all had trading bases in West Africa. It was at this time that tobacco and sugar were becoming important plantation crops in the Americas. Later, cotton became even more important than tobacco. The demand for labor increased greatly. Many more slaves were needed to plant and harvest the cotton crop. So the cruel Atlantic slave trade continued to grow.

During the seventeenth, eighteenth, and early nineteenth centuries, Europeans did not explore the center of Africa. For one thing, they were mainly interested in trade. Trade could be carried on at the coastal forts. Also, travel inland was dangerous. Tropical diseases killed most Europeans who stayed long in tropical Africa.

★ Find out about these diseases: malaria, blackwater fever, sleeping sickness, yellow fever. What insects carry these diseases? How are they controlled today?

In addition, the African rulers of the coastal kingdoms had grown rich and powerful by providing slaves to the Europeans. They were the **middlemen** in the slave trade. If the traders began rounding up slaves themselves, the coastal rulers would lose their share of profits. For this reason they discouraged the traders from going inland.

● What is the role of the middleman in trade? Which other African states you have studied grew powerful by being the middleman in trade?

The Abolitionist Movement

By the middle of the eighteenth century, many people in Great Britain and the United States were disturbed by the slave trade. Groups in both countries felt that slavery was wrong and that slaves should be freed. They wanted to end the slave trade for humanitarian reasons. They began the **abolitionist movement**— the drive to *abolish*, or stop, the slave trade and slavery. In the nineteenth century, this movement was successful.

Many people felt the slaves should be returned to their African homes. The governments of the United States and Great

THE REPUBLIC OF LIBERIA, WEST AFRICA.

vention for the purpose, and declared themselves a free and sovereign State, by the name and title of the "Republic of Liberia."

It must be remembered that Mr. Roberts at this time occupied the gubernatorial office. The birthday of the new republic was the 24th day of August, 1847, and a truly memorable day in her history. Its dawn was ushered in by the firing of cannon; at eleven o'clock

EX-PRESIDENT JOS. J. ROBERTS, OF LIBERIA.

the governor received from a committee of ladies the new and national flag of the republic, composed of six red and five white stripes alternately, with a single white star in the blue field, in presence of a large crowd of citizens.

On the 5th of October, the first election took place under the new Constitution, when J. J. Roberts was proclaimed President of the Republic for two years

PRESIDENTIAL MANSION, ASHMUN STREET, MONROVIA.

ward made two attacks on Bassa Cove, but each time were repulsed with severe loss.

the Liberians vanquishing a savage foe, which numbered at the lowest estimate not less than five thousand

hand of Divine Providence was on our side and we gloriously triumphed. * * *

"I exceedingly regretted the necessity of this campaign, but it could not be avoided. It will convince the aboriginal inhabitants of the ability of the Government to maintain the laws, and punish crime, wherever committed within its jurisdiction."

As a religious community, Liberia has been highly favored. About one-third of its entire immigrant population belongs to some Christian Church. There are

HON. JOHN SEYS, U. S. CONSUL GENERAL IN THE LIBERIAN REPUBLIC.

nearly thirty churches, which employ the service of between forty and fifty preachers.

The Methodist Episcopal Church has an important mission in Liberia. It is formed with a regular conference, composed of three presiding elders' districts, with circuits, stations and schools. This mission now embraces the whole territory, including the Maryland

---

Britain agreed to set up two new states in West Africa. These free states were to be settled by freed slaves from the Americas. The new states were named **Liberia** (lī bēr′ ē ə) and **Sierra Leone** (sē er′ ə lē ō′ nē).

- Locate Liberia and Sierra Leone on the map on page 72. Are they independent states today?

This solution, however, was not completely satisfactory. In most cases, the freed slaves from the Americas were not returned to their own homelands. Hundreds of freed slaves arrived in Liberia and Sierra Leone. However, these lands were not empty. The arrival of so many people upset the existing societies and economies. The new people were often resented by other Africans. The freed slaves were strangers in their new African homes. The free states needed money, government, and laws. Because they needed these things, they came under foreign control. Great Britain made Sierra Leone a **crown colony**. The United States gave aid to Liberia.

▶ What do you think the words *crown colony* mean?

Missionaries and Explorers

With the end of the slave trade, a new phase in African history began. The groups who had led the anti-slavery movement were mainly Christian. Many of these groups sent missionaries to Africa. They wanted to introduce Christian ideas and Western education. Their work in Africa led to an interest in exploring the interior of the continent. European governments began to finance explorers' expeditions.

★ Find out about these explorers and their discoveries: Henry Stanley, David Livingstone, Richard Burton, John Speke, Mungo Park.

As a result of these explorations, Europe learned of the vast resources that lay within Africa. Africa could supply raw materials for Europe's growing industries. It could also provide new markets for European goods. Europeans, then, became more interested in African raw materials and African markets. European nations began to take an imperialistic interest in Africa.

● How do you think Europe's industrial economy affected Africa's undeveloped economy? Give some reasons why an industrial revolution did not take place in Africa.

Henry Stanley. The explorers were not only important for their discoveries but also for providing Europe with a picture of African peoples and their cultures.

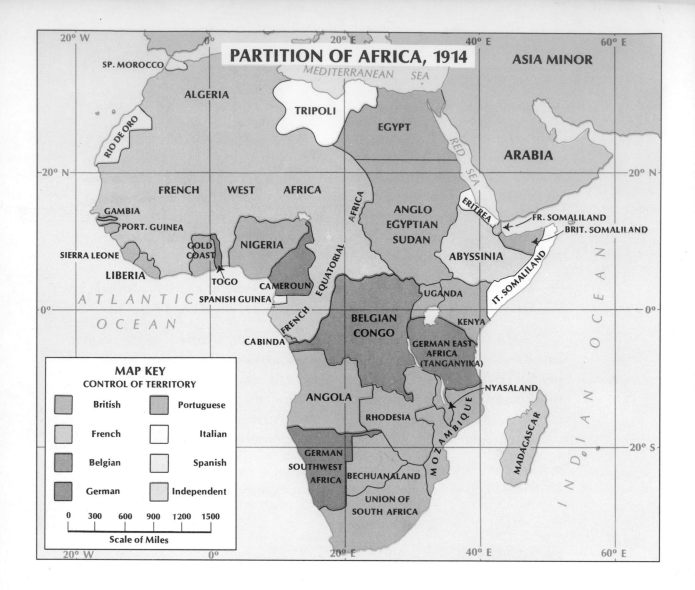

PARTITION OF AFRICA, 1914

MAP KEY
CONTROL OF TERRITORY

British
French
Belgian
German
Portuguese
Italian
Spanish
Independent

0   300   600   900   1200   1500
Scale of Miles

The Berlin Conference

In 1884, the European powers met in Berlin. They agreed to divide Africa into colonies. Great Britain, France, Germany, Portugal, Spain, Italy, and Belgium all had important interests in Africa. They all needed raw materials and markets. Each of these nations took control of a section of Africa. By 1914, almost all of Africa had been divided among European nations.

► Look at the map above showing the partition of Africa. Which parts of Africa were *not* involved in the partition?

● How did European exploration of Africa help to bring colonial rule?

● Why was Europe able to seize control of Africa?

The European powers divided Africa according to their own interests. They set up new territorial boundaries. The new boundaries often placed Africans of the same tribe in two different countries. They often united, under the same colonial rule, Africans of different tribes, who spoke different languages. Tribes that had been friendly were often separated. Tribes that had been enemies were often joined together.

- What problems would this present for colonial rulers? What problems would it create for Africans as they gained independence?

Patterns of Imperial Rule

Western imperialism in Africa went through several stages. First came traders seeking slaves and gold. They set up coastal trading posts. There the traders were often joined by missionaries. Soldiers were needed to protect the trading posts against raids. The trading posts became forts. Sometimes African tribes attacked the coastal forts. If that happened, the soldiers went inland to defeat the attacking tribe and restore peace. As more African lands and people came under European control, roads and railways were needed to move goods and soldiers. Africans supplied the labor for these building projects. As this expansion continued, some Africans lost their lands to Europeans. In some parts of Africa, Europeans came to settle on the land and farm it. Europeans also claimed the minerals and other resources they found.

There were generally two types of European government in Africa. One was the system used by France, Belgium, and Portugal. Its aim was to make Africans as European as possible. Educated Africans could earn the rights of French, Belgian, or Portuguese citizenship. They would then be considered the equal of any other European citizen. There were problems with this system. First, most Africans did not *want* to become European. Second, the necessary education was seldom provided by the colonial government.

- Why would Africans not want to become "European"?

Great Britain and Germany practiced another form of colonial rule. They set up a European form of government in their terri-

British colonial commissioners often met with African rulers to discuss problems of governing.

tories. They appointed their own officials to run them. In some places they allowed their own citizens to settle in Africa as farmers and businessmen. They kept all these people separate from the Africans.

Sometimes, the British tried to rule through the native government. They set up protectorates. More often, however, the British did the ruling themselves.

The coming of the Europeans destroyed traditional ways of life in Africa. The slave trade upset the development of West Africa for centuries. The impact of Western technology and capitalism ruined the old African social and economic systems.

▶ Why? What had happened when some African rulers acquired firearms?

By the end of the nineteenth century, almost all of Africa belonged to one European empire or another. Africans had European ways forced on them. In some ways they made rapid advances under colonial rule. Schools and medical care were introduced. Roads and railways were built. Communication networks were set up. A money economy developed in some areas, and industrial growth began. Africa had finally been drawn into contact with the outside world.

● How many kinds of imperialism can you find in the history of Western imperialism in Africa?

● How did European imperialism in Africa differ from imperialism in China and India? Explain.

The High Point of Western Imperialism

We have been studying a few examples of imperialism in the Modern Age. Many other examples could be given, both Western and non-Western. Western imperialism began in the sixteenth century with exploration, trade, and settlement. It reached its high point in the nineteenth century. By the end of that century most European colonies in the New World had become independent Western nations. Australia and New Zealand, too, were becoming Western nations. China was divided into spheres of economic influence. India was ruled by Britain. Africa was partitioned. The United States had taken over Hawaii and the Philippines. The United States, too, was getting more and more economic control in Latin America.

At the same time, the Russian Empire stretched across Asia. The Japanese Empire now included Korea and Formosa. Southeast Asia and the ancient Spice Islands were divided up among Britain, France, and the Netherlands.

In the twentieth century Western imperialism seemed to be ending. But it had left its mark in many lands. Especially interesting were the culture contacts that resulted from the mixing of Western and non-Western ideas. The next chapter will take a close look at an example of culture contact: the contact of British culture with the East African culture of the Ganda.

chapter 5

Western Culture and the Ganda People of Africa

The Impact of Western Culture on Non-Western Cultures

In this chapter, we shall study one society that felt the force of culture contact with the West. We shall see how Great Britain changed the kingdom of Buganda (bü gän' dä)..

In the Preface, culture contact was defined as "the things that happen when one culture or way of life comes into close touch with another and different culture." Think for a moment about this definition.

► What are some of the different forms culture contact can take?

We shall see only some of these forms of culture contact in the study of Buganda. As you read, try to pick out the types which took place there.

The Views of the Anthropologist and the Sociologist

All social scientists study man and his way of life. However, two groups of social scientists are particularly interested in the study of societies and culture contact. One group is the **anthropologists**

The traditional hut of the Ganda people is an interesting contrast to the modern parliament building in Uganda today.

(an thrə pol'ə jists). *Anthropology* (an' thrə pol'ə jē) is the study of man. Anthropologists study man's languages, his racial features, and his culture. They try to find out where man came from and what his history is. They compare one group of men to other groups. They ask in what ways these groups are alike. They also ask in what ways they are different. Anthropologists are especially useful in the study of culture contact. They help us find out about what cultures were like *before* they had any outside contact.

The other group of scientists is the **sociologists** (sō si ol'ə jists). The sociologist studies the ways men live together in organized groups. He studies *societies.* The sociologist also studies what happens when a culture comes into contact with other cultures. What are the good results of this contact? What are the bad results? What new culture is formed as a result of this contact?

The work of the anthropologist and sociologist often overlaps in this study of culture and societies. Much of our knowledge of the culture of Buganda comes from the studies of the anthropologist and the sociologist.

As you read about this culture, keep these social science questions in mind:

What was the culture of the people before their contact with the West?

What happened to the culture and the people after this contact? What was gained and what was lost in the course of contact?

What is the difference between a culture and a civilization?

The Natural Environment of Buganda

The Ganda are a people who live in the African kingdom of Buganda. The kingdom is now a part of the independent nation of Uganda (ü gän' dä).

Buganda is crossed by the equator. It lies on the northwest shores of Lake Victoria. The land along the lake is low tropical forest. In the interior of the country, the land changes to savanna, or grassland. Beyond the savanna lies a high, hilly plateau.

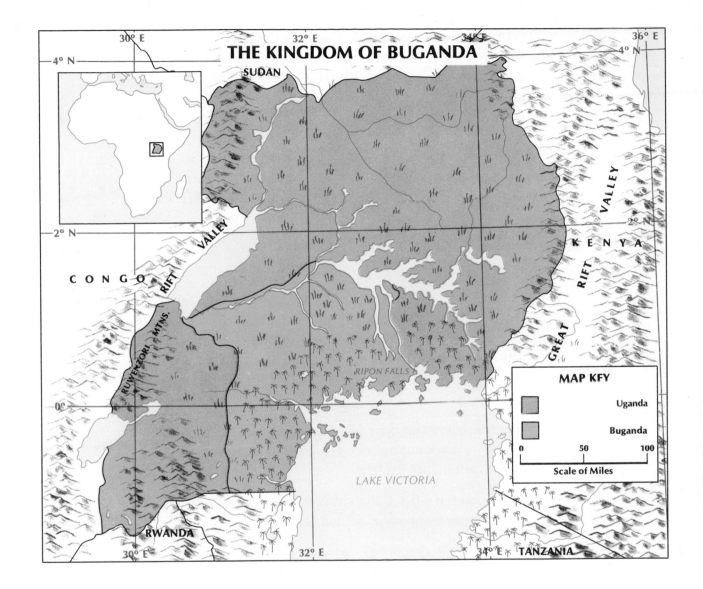

THE KINGDOM OF BUGANDA

SUDAN

CONGO

RIFT VALLEY

RUWENZORI MTNS.

RWANDA

RIPON FALLS

LAKE VICTORIA

KENYA

GREAT RIFT VALLEY

TANZANIA

MAP KEY

Uganda

Buganda

0   50   100

Scale of Miles

▶ Look at the map above. Find Lake Victoria, the Great Rift Valley, Ripon Falls and the Ruwenzori Mountains.

Lions, elephants, and antelope used to roam the grasslands. Today, most animals are in national parks. Brightly colored birds and many kinds of monkeys live among the trees and plants of the forest.

Buganda has two rainy seasons and two dry seasons. During the rainy seasons, precipitation is plentiful. Because the plateau is about 4,000 feet above sea level, the climate is not very hot. Most of the country has mild temperatures the year round.

Until the nineteenth century, Buganda was cut off from the outside world. It had strong natural defenses. The rivers were not easy to navigate. Thick jungles and swamps blocked the route to Africa's east coast.

The Ganda did not need to trade for food or goods. Their own farming supplied their needs. Bananas were their main crop. Bananas grow on tree-like plants. Because they are a tree crop, bananas do not need much land.

▶ Why is less land needed to grow tree crops than to grow field crops?

The Ganda lived in a good natural environment. The climate and soil gave an easy supply of food. So the Ganda did not need to develop an advanced technology. They did not have to conquer new lands to support their population. Their people were all members of the same tribe. It was easy for Buganda to grow into a unified kingdom.

● Discuss the advantages and possible disadvantages of a good natural environment. Is it sometimes good for people to have to struggle against their environment? Explain.

▶ Why did the Ganda have little contact with the outside world? Why didn't they need to develop an advanced technology?

● What advantages did Buganda have as a place to live? (Think of its physical features: landforms, altitude, Lake Victoria. Think of its climate.)

The Culture of the Ganda

Buganda does not have valuable mineral resources. There is not enough pasture land to graze cattle. The Ganda did not become traders or cattle herders. Instead, they settled on the high plateau where they farmed small plots of land.

The Ganda did not keep written records. We know very little about their early history. Probably, they came to Buganda many centuries ago.

The Ganda were better organized than most East African tribes. They had a strong central government, headed by a powerful king. They had a steady food supply, based on agriculture. However, the Ganda did not have a written language or a calendar. Although they had iron tools and weapons, they did not have either the plow or the wheel.

▶ Which social science helps us to learn about the culture and early history of the Ganda?

Political Organization: A Strong Monarchy

What made the Ganda strong was their system of government. Buganda was one of several tribal kingdoms that grew up in the region around Lake Victoria. It was not the largest or richest of these kingdoms. Yet Buganda quickly overtook the others in importance. This happened largely because of its strong government and powerful kings.

Farm land and farm labor were the main forms of wealth in the kingdom. To be a strong ruler, the king had to control the land and its produce. The importance of controlling the land led to a feudal type of government.

● What do we mean by a *feudal type of government?*

The king, or **kabaka** (kə bä' kə), ruled for life. Although he was not a god or priest to his people, the *kabaka* had a powerful hold over them. To his people, he stood for the strength and wealth of the state.

Men whose fathers or grandfathers had ruled as *kabaka* were called Princes of the Drum. From these princes a new *kabaka* was chosen. The choice was made by a council of elders.

Below the king were the important chiefs, or **bakunga** (bə kün' gə). They governed the largest land districts. The chiefs were responsible for certain jobs within their districts. They acted as judges and policemen. They built roads connecting their districts with the next higher ranking political district. They organized and led their people in war and in animal hunts. They were the link between the small villages and the royal capital.

The **bataka** (bə tä' kə), or lesser chiefs, were below the great chiefs. They were the heads of clans. These chiefs governed land that belonged to the clans.

Another important officer was the **katikkiro** (ka ti kē'rō), or prime minister. The *kabaka* also had a group of trusted personal followers, called the **batangole** (bə tan gō' li), or king's men. They served as a kind of palace guard.

The *kabaka's* mother and sister also had some political power. Each had her own royal lands and chiefs. All these people helped to govern Buganda, under the strong central rule of the *kabaka*.

THE STRONG CENTRAL GOVERNMENT OF THE GANDA

The King
or KABAKA

Kabaka's Advisors:
his mother, elder sister,
and council of chiefs

The Prime Minister
or KATIKKIRRO

Kabaka's Special Followers
the BATANGOLE

The Ten Chiefs of Counties
the BAKUNGA

About Thirty Heads of Clans
the BATAKA

Notice how all the power leads back to the kabaka.

The rest of the Ganda were either peasants or slaves. The peasants worked the land of their chief. They fought under him in wartime. Most slaves were people who had been captured in war. They had no rights. Most of them were farm workers or household servants.

Each peasant paid a tax of goods and services to his village chief. All the chiefs paid a tax to the *kabaka*. Many neighboring states also paid a tax to the kingdom of Buganda.

The Landholding System

Buganda was divided into ten large counties. These counties were divided into many smaller areas called districts. Each was ruled by a chief or sub-chief chosen by the *kabaka*. The *kabaka* had absolute power over these chiefs. He could transfer or dismiss them whenever he liked. When this happened, the land was passed on to the new chief. In this way, the *kabaka* kept the chiefs from becoming too powerful.

► In Buganda, land and position were not inherited. How did this keep any chief from getting too much power?

Landholding in Buganda was the key to power and wealth. Land determined one's **status**, or place in society. The chief held land because he was the chief. That was his status. The natives held their plots of land because they were the subjects of the chief. That was their status. Each of the Ganda knew his status. Each of the Ganda knew what was expected of him because of his status.

● Why was it necessary for the *kabaka* to control the land and its produce? How did this tend to make him an absolute ruler?

● Look up the word *status*. What determines the status you hold (you may have more than one)? What behavior is expected of you because of your status?

● Which system would give the *kabaka* more power: one in which he appointed chiefs, or one in which chiefs inherited their positions?

The Clans and the Family

Side by side with the governmental and land systems was the clan system. Each person was a member of the clan to which his mother belonged.

There were 30 to 40 clans in Buganda. Each clan was named after its **totem** (tō'təm). The totem was sacred. It was a certain animal or vegetable that clan members were forbidden to eat. There was the mushroom clan, the grasshopper clan, and the frog clan. The royal clan was the leopard clan.

Clan membership was important to the Ganda for many reasons. It gave them a strong sense of kinship. It was like belonging to a large family. The clans had certain rules. For example, all Ganda had to **outmarry**. That is, they could not marry anyone from their mother's or father's clan. However, the *kabaka* could marry a woman from any clan. His children became members of their mother's clan. Each clan hoped to have one of its women chosen as a *kabaka's* wife. If that happened, the next *kabaka* might be a member of their own clan.

Each clan elected its own leaders. However, the *kabaka* had to approve the choice. The clans owned their own lands, which usually were scattered throughout the kingdom. A clan member always had the right to use a piece of clan land for his home.

► Which do you think was older: the kinship clan system or the political system of Buganda? Why?

► How could the *kabaka* influence clan leadership, even though he did not appoint the clan heads?

Marriage was not practiced among the Ganda as it is in most Western cultures. The Ganda practiced **polygyny** (pə lij'ə nē). This means that a man could have several wives. A woman could leave her husband, if she chose to, and return to live with her parents. Children were often brought up by their relatives. Sometimes, sons were sent to live in the chief's household or the *kabaka's* palace. A boy who was raised in this way might one day become a powerful chief himself.

Daily Life and Religion

Most Ganda were farmers, but women did all the work of growing crops. The men had other things to do. Their main interests were politics and war. Buganda was often at war with other kingdoms. However, these wars were not fought to wipe out tribes, or to destroy their lands and crops. To the Ganda, war was a kind of game or sport. The winner collected slaves and tribute from the loser. The *kabaka* kept a large army and a fleet of war canoes, but he and his people were not especially interested in conquering new lands. They preferred to live quietly in their villages. Serious wars were fought only to protect their lands. The Ganda were never defeated in war. They remained independent.

The Ganda were skillful builders. Their houses were dome-shaped. Some of them were 50 feet tall. They were made of woven reeds on a framework of poles. Each family had one big house and several huts. There was a bathing hut and a cooking hut. There were sleeping huts for wives and children. Meals were often served by slaves. The food included a fish or meat stew,

bananas, sweet potatoes, and sugar cane. With their meal the Ganda drank beer brewed from bananas. Afterwards, they chewed coffee beans.

Both men and women were expert craftsmen. They wove a soft, strong cloth from the bark of the fig tree. Their reed baskets were so tightly woven that they held water. They also made musical instruments, including harps, drums, and trumpets. They were fine sailors, fishermen, and boat builders. Some of their war canoes were 70 feet long.

The Ganda dressed in long barkcloth robes. They often added a cape of antelope skin and bead necklaces. They did not scar their faces with clan markings, and they looked down upon other African tribes who did.

The Ganda religion was based on the worship of spirits. The chief god ruled the air and water. He blessed the tribe with wealth and children. He also protected sailors. Before setting out in their canoes, sailors threw bananas into Lake Victoria as an offering to him. The Ganda also worshipped the spirits of former *kabakas* and great chiefs. Slaves were often sacrificed to honor these ancestors.

● Look at the chart on page 87. Use it as a check list to review what you know about the culture of the Ganda.

86

QUESTIONS TO ASK ABOUT A CULTURE

1. GEOGRAPHY

What is the land like? What have men done to the land?

2. ECONOMICS

How are goods produced? How are goods exchanged or traded? How is money used? How are goods distributed?

3. RELIGION AND PHILOSOPHY

What do the people believe about God or the gods? What do they believe about the meaning of life? What do they believe about right and wrong? How do their beliefs affect their lives?

4. KNOWLEDGE, EDUCATION, AND THE ARTS

Have the people developed any new knowledge? What kind of knowledge do they think is important? What can we learn about them from their printing, sculpture, building, music, books?

5. POLITICAL SCIENCE

How are the people governed? Do they have laws?

6. SOCIOLOGY

Do the people live in groups such as the family? Are there rich men and poor men? Are there slaves?

7. HISTORY

Is there much change in the society? Is the society changing slowly or quickly?

The Arab Slave Trade Comes to Buganda

In 1844, Arab traders came to Buganda in search of slaves and ivory. Like many other African rulers, the *kabaka* saw a way to enrich himself by helping the Arabs. He led his people in raiding other tribes. The captured people were traded to the Arabs as slaves. The slave trade became so profitable that many Arabs settled permanently in Buganda. They provided the *kabaka* with firearms, silks, and jewelry. They introduced the Muslim religion. The Arabs also brought news from the outside world. They warned the *kabaka* of Europe's growing interest in central Africa.

● What were some of the major reasons for Western Europeans' interest in Africa?

The Coming of the Europeans

John Speke, a British soldier and explorer, was the first European to visit Buganda. Speke had come to Africa to find the source of the White Nile. He arrived in Buganda in 1862. He stayed for several months as the guest of Kabaka Mutesa I.

Mutesa (mü tā sə) was a strong and confident ruler. He was proud of his kingdom and his people. He was not afraid of outsiders. He was eager to meet the European explorer.

Speke exchanged gifts with the *kabaka*. He presented Mutesa with guns and ammunition, a telescope, a gold watch, rolls of cloth, and strings of beads. In return, Mutesa made him a gift of cattle and game, along with several porcupines and rats.

Mutesa was fascinated by his new weapons. He liked to walk around the palace grounds, shooting at birds. On these walks he was followed by his wives and attendants and the court musicians. Whenever the *kabaka* killed a bird, everyone would fall to his hands and knees, in honor of Mutesa's "magical powers."

Speke was impressed by the beauty and order of Buganda. He admired its people and its peaceful prosperity. However, he was horrified by the *kabaka's* cruelty and misuse of his power. Torture and human sacrifice were everyday events in Mutesa's court. Mutesa had his attendants beheaded for talking too loudly or for failing to open a door for him.

Explorers Speke and Grant learn about the Ganda people from Kabaka Mutesa.

To Speke, Mutesa's cruelty was a strange contrast to the Ganda culture that he admired. Mutesa, however, thought his actions proved his absolute power.

► Why would Mutesa feel that his actions proved his power?

Speke noticed the strong Muslim influence at court. This, together with Mutesa's cruelty, convinced him that the Ganda should learn about Christianity. Yet Speke was not able to bring Christianity to the Ganda. He died soon after his return to England. For many years after Speke, there was little British interest in Buganda.

The second Western explorer to visit Mutesa's court was Henry Stanley, who arrived in 1875. Stanley persuaded the British government to send Christian missionaries into the kingdom. A Protestant missionary arrived from England the next year, followed by a Catholic missionary from France.

At first, Mutesa was delighted with the missionaries. He invited them to live at his court and to hold Bible classes there. Mutesa himself never became either a Christian or a Muslim. Still, he allowed the missionaries to instruct and convert his subjects. Many Ganda soon became Christians.

● Many of the Ganda accepted Christianity easily. Give some reasons for this.

Mutesa had good reasons for being kind to the missionaries. He knew that the Christians came from two powerful European governments. He thought they would help him drive back an invading Egyptian army. He began to favor them over the Mus-

Mutesa and members of his court.

lims. However, when Mutesa realized that the missionaries could not supply him with soldiers and weapons, his favors to them ended.

The two Christian groups were very jealous of each other. Both, however, bitterly opposed the Muslims. Mutesa could not understand this religious conflict. He grew impatient with the missionaries and forced many of them to leave Buganda.

▶ Why did the *kabaka* at first favor the missionaries? Why did he turn against them?

● Why might religious conflict be hard for a Ganda to understand?

The spread of Christianity stopped under the rule of Mutesa's son, Mwanga. First, Mwanga became a Muslim. As a Muslim, he was expected to drive the Christians out of Buganda. He began to persecute all the Christians in the kingdom. However, Mwanga was not really afraid of Christianity. He was afraid that the Europeans wanted to take over his kingdom. There was some truth in this. By this time, the European powers were building empires in Africa. Great Britain, France, and Germany all wanted to control Buganda. They were interested in gaining power and land in Buganda. Each country sided with one of the religious groups. Each group tried to drive out the others.

A long period of civil war began. The Muslim Ganda fought with the Christian Ganda. The Ganda and the Europeans feared and distrusted each other. Now the chiefs, whose loyalty had always belonged to the *kabaka*, began to take sides with the religious groups. The power of the *kabaka* was weakened. The traditional kingdom began to fall apart.

● Explain in your own words how Western ideas affected the culture of the Ganda. How did they affect religion? Government? Social relations?

Buganda was still torn by civil war when Great Britain took over the government. The Imperial British East Africa Company (IBEA) had come to Buganda in 1890 to set up a trading company. However, the political unrest made it impossible for the company to carry on business.

In 1894, IBEA asked the British government for help. Great Britain established a *protectorate government* for Buganda and three neighboring kingdoms—Bunyoro, Toro, (tō′ rō) and Ankole (äng kō′ lā). These territories are part of present-day Uganda.

● What would a protectorate government be like? What would it try to do?

● Compare the actions of the IBEA with the actions of the British East India Company in India.

The 1900 Agreement

In 1900 the British and the Ganda signed the agreement that made Buganda a British protectorate. The 1900 Agreement was the basis of British-Ganda relations for more than 50 years.

The most important part of the Agreement was about land-holding. About half the land in Buganda was given to the *kabaka* and the most important chiefs. The remainder went to Great Britain. The *kabaka's* council made the land division. This meant that the Ganda were able to choose good, fertile land.

Not all Englishmen favored the Protectorate. Here, a Member of Parliament suggests that "In Uganda there is absolutely no prospect of commerce. . . ."

However, this arrangement weakened the *kabaka's* authority. The chiefs no longer depended on him for their land or their power. Under the Agreement, they became a landowning aristocracy in their own right.

The 1900 Agreement also ignored the land rights of the clans. The clan elders lost their land and their power. They had to become tenants on the estates of the great chiefs. The traditional power of the clan and the *kabaka* was greatly weakened by the Agreement.

In spite of these problems, the British protectorate worked well. The British did not try to run the country themselves. Instead, they ruled *through* the native rulers. This form of government is called indirect rule.

● Why might indirect rule in the protectorate be more successful than direct rule?

The British Protectorate

The British did not try to make the protectorate just like their own government. Instead, they based it on the kind of laws and customs the Ganda had always had. This made the task of the new government easier. Later, when Uganda became independent, it made it easier for Britain to withdraw and leave an orderly government. At the same time, however, it gave Buganda a special position. The other three kingdoms in Uganda had to accept Buganda's form of government. But when Uganda became independent, Buganda was forced to accept equal standing with the states that had formerly paid tribute to it.

● Why were the British wise to base colonial government on the existing Ganda government? What problems did it solve? What problems did it create?

From Subsistence Farming to Cash Crops

At first, the British planned to develop plantations in Buganda. However, the first few plantations were not very successful. Soon the British realized that the Ganda were growing cotton on their own lands as a cash crop. They were doing quite well, too. The government encouraged cotton growing by individuals. Later, coffee growing was introduced so that the economy would not be dependent on a single crop. Today, Uganda is one of the leading coffee producers in the world.

● What are the dangers of a one-crop economy?

Buganda never attracted many white settlers. There was not much chance for Europeans to grow rich or powerful there. Today, 99 out of every 100 persons in Buganda are African.

Between 1895 and 1900, many important changes took place in Buganda. First, the civil and religious wars were ended for good. Then the government abolished slavery. Construction began on a railway to connect Buganda with the east coast of Africa. Finally a tax-supported school system was established in Buganda.

▶ How would the railway help Buganda's economy? How would it encourage cash crops?

Many other changes have taken place in Buganda since its contact with Western culture. Buganda is still mainly an agricultural nation. But now the Ganda men, not the women, are the planters and cultivators. They are the ones responsible for family earning. The missionaries showed the Ganda the importance of education. Today, teachers cannot be trained fast enough to meet the country's needs. The missionaries were successful in another way, too. Today, eight out of every ten Ganda are Christians. Both missionaries and British officials opened all sorts of jobs to the Ganda. Thus, even though most Ganda are farmers, other opportunities of work do exist.

● The British government tried to interfere as little as possible in the culture of Buganda. Yet many cultural changes did occur. What were they? Were they good or bad? How would you describe the culture contact in Buganda? Was Ganda society changed deeply by contact with the West?

★ Report on one of these men: Frederick Lugard (lü gärd'), Kabaka Mutesa I, Milton Obote (ō bō tā).

The Ganda Today

The British created in Buganda a successful protectorate. They used the existing government of Buganda. However, they also tried to force Ganda methods on the other kingdoms in the protectorate. These other peoples distrusted the Ganda.

Today, the Ganda remain the most important single group in Uganda. Kampala (käm pä' lä), the national capital, is located in Buganda. It is the heart of the nation's economic and political life. It is the communications center for the whole country.

Money income in Buganda is two to ten times greater than anywhere else in the country. Many people from other parts of Africa come to Buganda, looking for jobs and education. Many settle there permanently. The Ganda are in danger of becoming a minority in their own land. The Ganda are used to their favored position. They want to have a major role in the government of Uganda. But they feel that they are different from the other peoples in the new nation. Although they have been able to benefit from Western ways, they have kept their own culture. Thus, they have found it difficult to unite with the rest of Uganda. They have tried several times to secede, or break away, from the new nation. Let us see what happened after Uganda became independent.

Uganda was declared an independent nation on October 9, 1962. In 1963, Milton Obote, the prime minister, persuaded the voters to elect the *kabaka* of Buganda as president of the new nation. This idea was unpopular outside Buganda. However, it was necessary. It was the only way to draw the Ganda into the federation of Uganda. The peaceful unity of the new nation did not last long. Early in 1966, the Ganda rebelled against Obote. With the national army, Obote put down the rebellion. He declared himself president. The Ganda then tried to drive the federal government out of the capital, Kampala. Obote sent his army to attack the *kabaka's* palace. A fierce battle followed. Several hundred Ganda were killed. The *kabaka* was forced to flee to London.

In order to break the power of the Ganda, Obote then put an end to the kingdom of Buganda altogether. He divided it into four districts. Each district is headed by an official of the national government. However, many Ganda remained loyal to the exiled *kabaka*. They still believed in Ganda unity.

How would you answer the question on the blackboard?

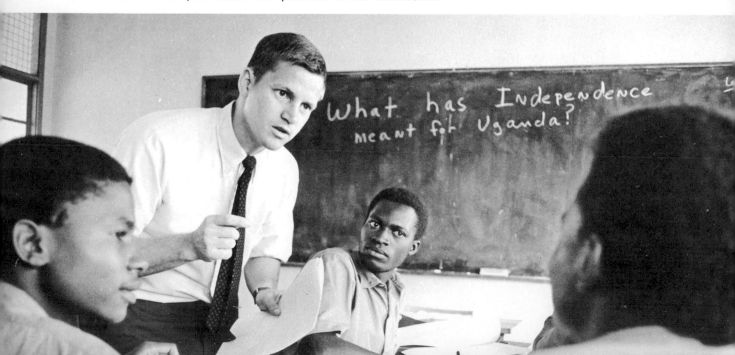

In 1969, Kabaka Edward Mutesa II died in London, after three years in exile. He had never returned to his kingdom.

● Why would the Ganda have trouble accepting the overthrow and exile of the *kabaka*? Why was it hard for them to join the new nation?

● How does the recent history of Uganda help us to understand the problems resulting from *the uniting of different tribes and peoples under an imperial power*?

★ What happened in Nigeria after that nation gained independence? Are the relations of the Ibo (Biafrans) with other peoples in Nigeria similar in any way to the relations of the Ganda with other peoples in Uganda? Was the treatment of the Ganda by Obote better or worse than the treatment the Biafrans received?

Culture Change

Great Britain differed from Buganda in many ways. First, Great Britain had a highly developed industrial economy and an advanced technology. It had a different system of government and religion. It also had wealth and power. The Western nation was powerful enough to force change on the less advanced people.

Many of these changes brought benefits and improvement. Constitutional government replaced tribal rule by the *kabaka*. New crops were encouraged to put the farming economy on a sounder basis. Scientific and medical knowledge brought health and greater prosperity to the people.

However, not every change was an advantage to the people who received it. Some Western ideas tended to weaken the native culture and society. The traditional ways of life were destroyed. People lost their independence as they came under foreign rule. Also, Westerners did not always recognize the value of the way of life they were working to replace. They failed to realize that many Western beliefs and practices were not suitable, or did not make sense, to other people.

★ Make a list of the good and bad results of Western imperialism and culture contact for the Ganda and their neighbors in Uganda.

chapter 6

Nationalism, Democracy, and Other Controlling Ideas

Some Ideas That Control Our Lives Today

Human societies are controlled partly by ideas. Men, women, and children usually try to live up to their ideas of what is right and wrong. They first learn these ideas from the society they live in. People also use their own powers of reason to learn right from wrong. But a good starting point for a person is to learn the controlling ideas of the society in which he lives.

● What great sets of controlling ideas have you already studied? Review some of these ideas. In which regions of the world are Islamic ideas most important? In which regions of the world is Buddhism strong?

Ideas are not fixed forever. Men keep thinking about ideas. They look for new ways to solve the old problems of how to lead good lives and how to be free—how to avoid evil and slavery.

Ideas are passed along to other men. One set of ideas may lead to another. Christianity stemmed from Judaism. Christianity, mixed with Greco-Roman ideas, helped to develop Western European culture. In Western Europe, disagreements in Christendom brought the Reformation and Protestantism.

By the nineteenth century, the Industrial Revolution had brought great change to men's lives. It had also brought problems. Many men began to think about these problems. Some believed that the way to solve these problems was by making society better. They made different plans for this. A plan to remake or reshape society is known as an **ideology** (id'e äl'ə jē). An ideology usually begins as a set of ideas. At first, these ideas may be believed only by one man or a few men. But other men may accept this ideology and then follow it. An ideology does not begin as a controlling idea. It may become one if many men believe and follow it.

- Look up the word *ideology*. You will see that the difference between controlling ideas and ideologies is not always clear.

- What ideas and ideologies were used by the French revolutionaries and Napoleon?

★ Read the following lines from Arthur O'Shaughnessy's poem "The Music Makers." How do they show the power of words and ideas over human societies?
    One man with a dream, at pleasure
    shall go forth and conquer a crown;
    and three with a new song's measure
    can trample an Empire down.

In nineteenth-century Europe, certain new ideas and ideologies became very, very powerful. They are still among the controlling ideas of the world today. They have spread to every civilized society. These powerful ideas are nationalism, democracy, humanitarianism, socialism, and communism.

We shall see how many of these ideas spread to other societies in different parts of the world. We shall see how men acted under the influence of these ideas and ideologies. But first, let us make sure that we know what the words mean.

●   Look up the words *conservative* and *liberal*. You may have read about them in the discussion of the French Revolution in *The Challenge of Change*.

Nationalism

Of all the controlling ideas in the world today, nationalism is one of the most powerful. **Nationalism** is the feeling of pride and loyalty that people feel for their nation.

●   Make sure you know the difference between *nationality* and *nationalism* and between *humanity* and *humanitarianism*. These terms are very important. You should learn to use them correctly.

We have seen in *The Human Adventure* that people have given their loyalty to many kinds of communities and groups. They have also been loyal to certain individuals. They have been loyal to their clan or tribe, their city-state or feudal lord, their king, or their religious group. Throughout history the loyalties of people have changed. During the eighteenth century more and more people began to believe in the idea of nations.

We have seen how nations began to appear in Western Europe 500 years ago. As more and more people began to settle in one area, they began to share their cultures. England, France, and Spain each had its own language, its own literature, and its own customs. Each nation had its own strong government with strong armed forces. The English, French, and Spanish people began to think of themselves as members of a nation. They began to feel loyal to their nation. Thus, the idea of nationalism arose.

In some parts of the world today, political leaders are trying hard to make their people become nationalistic. It is not always easy. Many societies are still *tribal* and not *national* in their thinking. This means that the peoples' first loyalty goes to their family and tribal group and not to the nation they live in. Some nation-states include groups with different languages and customs. In spite of these difficulties, political leaders everywhere want to develop the idea of nationalism in their countries. They want the loyalty of the people to go first to the nation-state. They feel this is one way to help their nations become strong and united.

- How does this remind you of your study of the growth of Uganda?

- Was nationalism in the United States more difficult to develop than nationalism in England or France? Why or why not?

- Do you think that the idea of nationalism might conflict with the idea of imperialism? Explain.

Democracy

Democracy comes from two Greek words meaning "rule by the people." It means that all the people share in the government of their society.

The idea of democracy as a form of government is very old. It has also been combined with other forms of government.

Democracy was tried in classical Athens and in other Greek city-states. Democracy, as used by the Greeks, meant that all adult free men were to share in making decisions. This was done in meetings of the Assembly. All citizens were free to attend the Assembly. It was their duty to take part in the governing of their city. All issues were decided by voting. The people accepted the choices made by the majority of the voters. This is the idea of majority rule. This form of government is called **direct democracy.**

Later, the Romans developed a different form of government. This was a mixed, *republican* government. This type of government combined several different things. It had an assembly where the people voted. This was very much like the Assembly of Athens. It had magistrates, or important officials, at the head of the government. It had a selected group of men, the Senate, to discuss things and advise the leaders of Rome. In such a mixed government, the power is divided so that the majority does not always have its way. The rights of the minority are also respected.

A republican government is sometimes a *representative government.* In this type of government, the people elect representatives to make decisions for them. As communities grew bigger and bigger, it was impossible for all of the people to meet together to make decisions. The people, then, had to elect represent-

GRECIAN DEMOCRACY IS THE CENTER POINT FROM WHICH OTHER FORMS OF DEMOCRACY DEVELOPED.

atives to make decisions for them. Many times, they also made a constitution, or set of rules for government.

The idea of representative government became very important in the Middle Ages. The English Parliament is an example of representative government. However, in the Middle Ages, most people did not believe in the democracy of the Greeks. They did not believe that all the citizens of the community should be allowed to vote or to take part in the government.

After the American and French Revolutions, however, many men began to think seriously about the way they were being governed. The state was no longer thought of as the king's state. It was the people's state. Men wanted to form governments where most people could share in the governing of the society.

The idea of democracy—of people sharing in government—became popular again. Democracy began to mean more than just the rule of the majority. The ideas of Greek democracy, Roman mixed government, and the representative tradition of the

Voting — a key to democratic government. Voting is an important way for people to participate in the governing of their society.

Middle Ages were combined to make a new definition of democracy—the **representative, constitutional republic**. This meant that all the people would share in their government through their elected representatives. It meant that there would be guaranteed rights for every citizen in the form of a constitution. It meant also that the power in government was divided. The majority could not do everything it liked. The rights of the minority were also respected.

This new meaning of democracy meant that all men were equal before the law. The laws of a country would be the same for every man. Each man had to obey the law whether he was a king, a farmer, or a merchant. All men had certain rights. The French Declaration of the Rights of Man talked about this new idea of democracy. It promised equal rights and equal opportunities to all men. For many people, the American Declaration of Independence was the best declaration of democratic ideals:

> We hold these Truths to be self-evident, that all Men are created equal, that they are endowed by their Creator with certain unalienable Rights [rights which cannot be taken away], that among these are Life, Liberty, and the Pursuit of Happiness.

The Constitution of the United States showed that it was really possible for many people to share in government. During the late eighteenth century, more and more people in Europe and the Americas began to favor democracy. They wanted to have some say in the governing of their nation. They wanted to have constitutions that gave all people certain rights.

▶ *All men have certain rights.* Explain what this means.

● Might "democracy, meaning rule of the majority" be opposed to "democracy, meaning equal rights for all"? Explain.

● In a country where the majority of the people were poor and unhappy, might democratic government lead to revolution? Explain.

● Can you see the connection between nationalism and democracy? Why must rule by the people or by the majority be based on common loyalties and patriotism?

Humanitarianism

Humanitarianism, the idea of men helping other men, was not a new idea in the nineteenth century. It was an idea that had long been taught by many religions.

Humanitarianism was especially important in the nineteenth century. It is important in our own century, too. Industry, science, and political revolutions had brought great changes and many problems. Humanitarianism was one way men hoped to solve some of these problems.

● Name some of the social problems of the Industrial Revolution.

People began to think that poverty was not always the fault of the poor, and it was everyone's responsibility to help improve the social conditions of their cities.

For the first time in human history, men in every part of the world began to learn about the whole human race. Production increased in industrial countries. Nations that were industrially well developed began to want to help less fortunate peoples. It became possible to help the poor to live better.

All sorts of humanitarian movements began. Missionaries went all over the world. In Britain and the United States, societies were formed to end the slave trade and abolish slavery. Men and women worked to change unfair criminal laws and poor prison conditions. Some people devoted themselves to providing better education for more people. Others devoted themselves to the improvement of hospitals and to care of the insane.

Nationalism, political revolutions, wars, and great discoveries are all very exciting. Sometimes they push the less exciting things out of history books. It is easy to forget the effect of many thousands of acts of kindness and concern during these same periods of great change.

- See if you can name some humanitarian efforts before the nineteenth century.

- Is humanitarianism a powerful idea in the world today? Give some examples.

★ Find out something about the ideals of charity and kindness in any one of the world's major religions. Compare your report with reports on other religions.

Socialism and Communism

Humanitarianism was one way of dealing with the problems and hopes during a time of great change. Two other ways of solving these problems were suggested. These were the ways of **socialism** or of **communism**. These two ideologies started in the first half of the nineteenth century. They did not become powerful controlling ideas until our own century.

What is a basic idea shared by socialism and communism? It is that all the people should own all the **means of production** (land, machines, factories) in a country. This means that the government owns all these things for the good of the people. In this way, the government can plan to produce what the people need and can give each person a fair share of the wealth of the nation.

The idea that the government could own and control most of the means of production was not new. Governments had done that many times in history. Modern socialism added two new ideas. The first was that, in a democratic government, all the people could share in the ownership of the means of production. The second was that a democratic government could distribute goods equally among the whole population. Socialism seemed to be another answer to the problems of change brought by the Industrial Revolution.

Many people thought the idea of socialism was foolish. How could everyone really own all the means of production? If the government gave out the goods equally, would people work hard enough? How could the politicians in control of the government be kept from giving themselves unfair shares? Who would save money to make more machines and factories? What about people who had worked hard and saved money to buy their own factories or farms? Would they have to hand their property over to the government when the majority voted for socialism?

Karl Marx, a nineteenth-century German philosopher, had ideas about socialism. He thought that people would never hand their property over to the government unless they were forced to do so. Marx developed a new ideology—the ideology of communism.

The new working class that grew during the Industrial Revolution was struck by poverty. Many factory workers were poor and overworked. They were sometimes unemployed. Marx said that private property was the cause of this poverty. He said that people who owned land and factories would have their property taken away from them. The members of the working class would use force to do this. These workers would be organized like the Paris workers at the time of the terror in the French Revolution. They would be led by Communists. Communists are people who share Marx's ideas. Communists would understand when to strike at and destroy those people who owned the means of production. Those who own the means of production are called **capitalists**.

On this collective farm in a Communist country, many families work together. The land, houses, and farm machines are owned by the state.

There is a big difference between socialism and communism. This difference still remains. Some people believe in **democratic socialism**. This means that socialism will come by peaceful, lawful voting. They generally think that a person who owns capital should be paid when his capital is turned into public property. Communists, however, are sure that this peaceful method is useless. They believe that power and property must be seized and held by force. Communists believe that the rich and poor are at war with one another. When the poor win this war between classes, a Communist government will be set up.

In the United States today, people keep thinking and arguing about these ideas. For example, most Americans today believe that a government should not *own* the means of production. But many think that the government should *regulate* some of the means of production and commerce. Others believe that government control and regulation should be as limited as possible. We can see that these ideas which began in the nineteenth century are still being thought about in our world today.

- Make sure that you know the meaning of *capital.* Who owns capital in a socialist or communist state? Who owns capital in the United States?

- Might democratic socialism take away certain rights from citizens? What rights?

- How would a Communist revolution affect the lives of ordinary citizens?

- Many citizens in the United States seem more suspicious of Communists than of democratic socialists. Can you explain why?

★ Do we have anything like democratic socialism in the United States? Do we have anything like communism? Does the federal government regulate or own any of the means of production or commerce? Explain.

★ Under what conditions would you expect many people to become socialists or to support communism?

★ Is competition between producers a good thing? Why or why not? Is there competition under socialism or communism?

A Socialist Thinker and Doer: Robert Owen

The Industrial Revolution had brought many problems for the workers. Many men wanted to solve these problems. They began to plan new factory systems in which all workers would be happy. Frenchmen, Englishmen, Americans, and Germans made many of these socialist plans for factories. Most of these plans were just dreams. But one socialist thinker—Robert Owen—put his ideas into practice.

Robert Owen was one of the first men to make a fortune in the British cotton industry. He thought that the living conditions of factory workers could be much better. He believed that workers should be well fed, well clothed, and well housed. Only then, he thought, would they work hard and well. Owen formed a plan to make a better society. He experimented with his ideas in the New Lanark (lan'erk) Mills in Scotland. There he built a community. He thought that this community could be used as an example for other people to make communities. Such a community is called a *model community*. At New Lanark, Owen raised wages. He shortened working hours. He built better housing. He allowed space for gardens and trees.

● Compare the situation in the Lanark community with that shown in the drawing of the mill town in Lancashire (lang' kə shər). Which would be the healthier place to live in? Why?

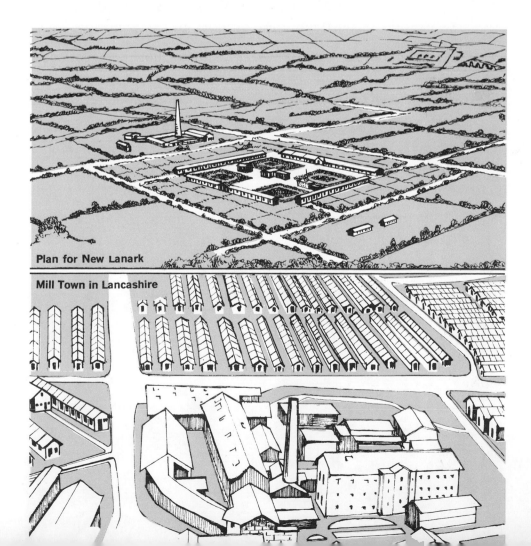

Plan for New Lanark

Mill Town in Lancashire

Soon the Lanark community was working well. Owen arranged for workers to share in the ownership of the mills. He also began a public school system which was later copied in England. Workers bought what they needed at a company store. Thus the owners of the village provided for all the workers' needs.

- Would you like to live in a village like New Lanark? Explain.

- Could Owen's plan solve all the problems of the workers? Why or why not?

- How would living in a community founded on socialist principles change your present life? Would you like it better or not so well?

Other socialist planners were not as successful as Robert Owen. Even Owen failed later on when he tried to set up a model community in the United States. This was at New Harmony, Indiana. The model community at New Harmony failed when the workers would not do their share of work in the factories.

- What would probably be the weakness of socialist communities in which every person was expected to do equal work and share all the products equally?

★ Find out more about Robert Owen and the early socialists. Some of them were: Charles Fourier (fü ryā′) and Louis Blanc (blän) [French]; John Humphrey Noyes [American]. Find out about an American model community, Brook Farm.

★ Find out more about Karl Marx and his friend, Friedrich Engels (eng′ əls).

Robert Owen

Karl Marx

HOW CONTROLLING IDEAS AFFECTED MEN'S LIVES IN NINETEENTH-CENTURY EUROPE

We have seen some controlling ideas which grew strong in the nineteenth century. Let us look at the way they affected men's lives at that time. The story is very complicated. Sometimes these ideas worked together. Sometimes they competed with one another.

Nationalism in Nineteenth-Century Europe

The most powerful controlling idea in Europe in the nineteenth century was nationalism. Many people in Europe wanted to live in a state made up only of people of the same nationality. A nationality group is a group of people sharing the same traditions and culture. Yet many states in Europe were made up of people of many nationalities.

The Congress of Vienna met in 1815 after the defeat of Napoleon. There the statesmen divided the peoples and lands of most of Western Europe into many countries. These men did not like the new idea of "nation" and "citizen." They believed in government by kings. They were also concerned about keeping the balance of power. As they redrew the map of Europe, they grouped together peoples of different nationalities, histories, and cultures.

- How might the separation of peoples of the same nationality and culture aid in keeping the balance of power?

As the years passed, the idea of nationalism grew stronger in Europe. It became especially strong in four areas: in Italy, in the Austrian Empire, in Germany, and among the Polish people. These areas had all been affected by the decisions of the Congress of Vienna.

The Italians had been divided into many states. Some of these states were under Austrian rule. Others were governed by kings and princes.

The Austrian government ruled many peoples who were not Austrian. Those peoples had very different histories. They spoke many different languages.

The people of Germany were also not united. They spoke the same language, but they were divided among many rulers. Few of these rulers allowed the people any share in government.

The idea of nationalism was not at work only in Western Europe. In Eastern Europe, most of the Polish people were ruled by Russia, the large country to the east of Poland. But the Polish people had a feeling of Polish nationalism. They dreamed of an independent Polish nation. They wanted freedom from Russian rule.

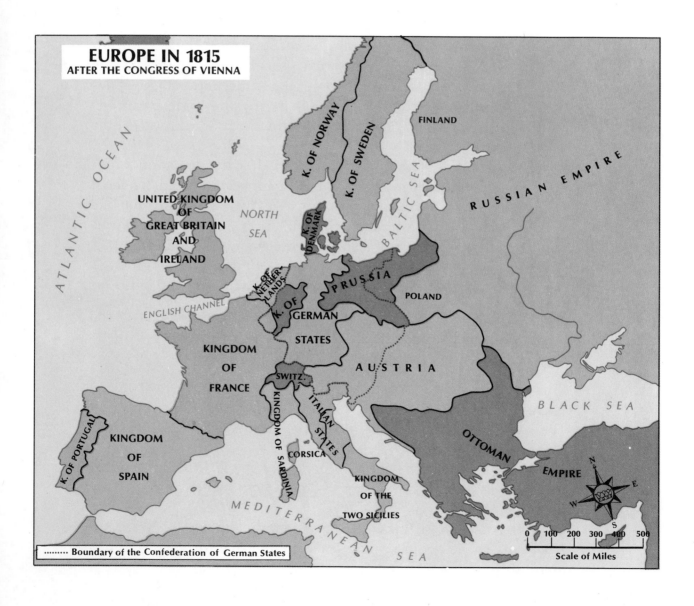

EUROPE IN 1815
AFTER THE CONGRESS OF VIENNA

ATLANTIC OCEAN

K. OF NORWAY

K. OF SWEDEN

FINLAND

RUSSIAN EMPIRE

UNITED KINGDOM OF GREAT BRITAIN AND IRELAND

NORTH SEA

BALTIC SEA

K. OF DENMARK

K. OF NETHERLANDS

PRUSSIA

POLAND

ENGLISH CHANNEL

K. OF GERMAN STATES

KINGDOM OF FRANCE

AUSTRIA

SWITZ.

KINGDOM OF SARDINIA

ITALIAN STATES

BLACK SEA

K. OF PORTUGAL

KINGDOM OF SPAIN

CORSICA

KINGDOM OF THE TWO SICILIES

OTTOMAN EMPIRE

MEDITERRANEAN SEA

N
W E
S

0 100 200 300 400 500

·········· **Boundary of the Confederation of German States**

Scale of Miles

During the nineteenth century, many of these national groups tried to gain their independence. They wanted to form nations with the people who shared the same history and culture. They wanted also to share in the governing of these nations.

► Look at the maps on these pages showing the political divisions of Europe in 1815 and 1871. Which nation-states were already unified in 1815? Which nation-states had been added by 1871?

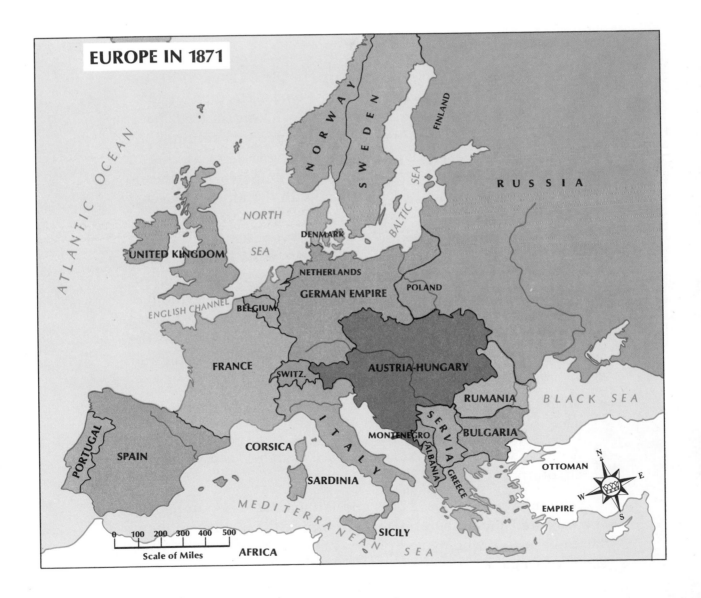

EUROPE IN 1871

Two Case Studies of Controlling Ideas at Work

We cannot try to follow every nationalistic and democratic movement in nineteenth-century Europe. We are going to study two examples of important movements in Europe. The first of these is an example of a movement in which several controlling ideas were at work together. This movement is the Revolution of 1848 in France. The second movement is an example in which nationalism was the most important controlling idea. This is the movement to form the nation-state of Italy.

The Revolution of 1848 in France

After the defeat of Napoleon Bonaparte in 1815, Louis XVIII, the brother of Louis XVI, became king of France. He died in 1824. His brother Charles X became the next French king. In 1830, many Frenchmen were tired of Charles X. These people overthrew his government. They chose Louis-Philippe (lü ē fə lēp') as king of France. Louis-Philippe was a **constitutional monarch**. This means that his powers were limited. He ruled with the aid of an elected legislature.

Between 1830 and 1848, there was rapid industrial growth in France. This Industrial Revolution brought with it many problems for the workers. At times, many workers were unemployed. The big cities, like Paris, were overcrowded with people who had no jobs. Many of the unemployed workers began to lean toward the ideas of socialism. They wanted the government to own the factories. They wanted the government to tax wealthy people and to give work and wages to the unemployed.

- What is "unemployment compensation" or "unemployment insurance"?

- Is it right for government to provide money to help people who are out of work? Why or why not?

The middle class merchants and farmers were also unhappy. They wanted more share in the government. But they thought that only people who owned property should be allowed to vote. They were against socialism.

The Uprising. *Factors such as poverty, poor living conditions, and unemployment frustrate men and lead them to seek change.*

There was also a group of revolutionaries called **radicals**. Radicals believe that society should be changed completely. They believe that these changes should be made quickly. Sometimes they use violence to make the changes they want.

By 1848, many Frenchmen believed that Louis-Philippe could not solve the many problems brought by the Industrial Revolution. Late in February 1848, groups of workers and students gathered in Paris. They wanted to show that they were unhappy with the government of Louis-Philippe. They demonstrated against it. Barricades were set up in the street, and fighting between workers and soldiers began. Within a few days, workers were in control of the city of Paris. Louis-Philippe's government lost control. The king fled to England. Louis-Philippe was the last French king. A temporary government was set up and elections were planned.

But the Revolution of 1848 in France was not over. Various groups began to struggle for control of the government. Bloody street fighting took place between these groups. What were the reasons behind the revolution of February 1848?

► This revolution was not one of nationalism. Why would there be no need to start a nationalistic revolution in France?

Was this a revolution for democracy? It was, in part. What did the revolutionaries want? All of them wanted some form of democracy. However, democracy may mean different things to different people. Most Frenchmen wanted a republican form of government. But they all did not agree on how much democracy they should have. As we have seen, some wanted all Frenchmen to have the right to vote. Some wanted only property owners to have this right.

▶ Which groups of Frenchmen wanted votes for everyone? Which groups wanted only some people to be allowed to vote?

Some Frenchmen, especially the unemployed workers, wanted socialism. They thought socialism would be a way to solve their problems of unemployment and poverty.

So what was the revolution all about? Some Frenchmen saw it as a democratic revolution. Some saw it as a socialist revolution. As you can see, two great controlling ideas were at work together in France in 1848. These two controlling ideas were democracy and socialism.

● Which groups in society would probably want socialism? Which would not want it? Here are a few groups to think about: factory owners, bankers, farmers, factory workers, army officers, unemployed men.

● Do all people in the same group in society always want the same things in government? When might everyone in one group want the same things?

After the February Revolution of 1848, the radicals and the workers joined together in order to help to get the idea of socialism into the government. They organized *national workshops* to help unemployed workers.

In April 1848, elections were held, and a majority of nonsocialists were elected to the National Assembly. Many property owners in the cities and in the farm regions were afraid of socialist ideas. They were afraid they would lose their property. They wanted to close the national workshops. They voted against the socialists.

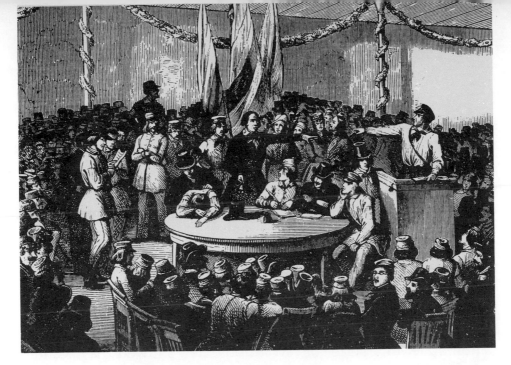

French university students discuss ways to help France.

The workers organized a protest march against the new government. The anti-socialists were determined to crush the protest. Bloody fighting broke out again. The soldiers of the government put down the workers' revolt.

When new elections were held, the voters elected Napoleon's nephew, Louis-Napoleon Bonaparte, president of the Second Republic. Louis-Napoleon promised to restore order to France. Two years later he made himself president for life. A year later, he announced that he was "Emperor Napoleon III of France." He was now a dictator. The Second Republic was over. The Second Empire had begun.

Within three years, what had started out as a democratic revolution, or maybe a socialistic revolution, had ended in a dictatorship.

- Why do revolutions often end up in military dictatorships?

- Explain why many people in France (many of whom could not read) were against socialism. Explain why they voted for the magic name "Napoleon Bonaparte" in the election for president.

- Would France have become a military dictatorship if the farmers and businessmen had not been afraid of socialism?

★ Find out why Louis-Napoleon called himself Napoleon III. Who was Napoleon II?

The Italian People Become the Nation-State of Italy

We have seen earlier that Napoleon I made many conquests. Among these were many states in the Italian peninsula. The empire of Napoleon I collapsed in 1814. The Italian states came again under the domination of Austria. In all there were nine different states. Each of these was ruled separately and undemocratically. Most of the rulers of these states were under the power of the Austrians.

Many people in these states felt a strong sense of Italian nationalism. They resented the control of the Austrians. They desired to unite the states of the Italian peninsula into a new nation-state. In a series of revolutions they showed they wanted to be free from Austrian rule.

To help make the nation-state of Italy, different leaders worked in different ways. One was the Italian writer Giuseppe Mazzini (jü zep'pe màt sē'nē). Mazzini liked the ideas of democracy. He wanted Italy to be united and ruled by a republican government. He formed a club for those who wanted a revolution against Austrian rule. This club was called *Young Italy*. Through this club he hoped to spread the idea of Italian nationalism.

One young man, Giuseppe Garibaldi (jü zep'pe gä rē bäl'dē) heard about *Young Italy*. He, too, believed that Italians should be united in a nation-state. In 1834, Garibaldi made a plan with Mazzini to start a revolution to free the Italian states. Garibaldi's plan was found out. He was captured and condemned to death. But he escaped. He went to Latin America. He helped the Latin Americans in their revolutions against Spain. But always he dreamed of coming back to his native Italy. He dreamed of the day when Italy would be united.

While Garibaldi was in Latin America, he had many adventures. He proved himself to be a man of great courage. He was a good soldier. He organized a small army of excellent soldiers. This small army was known as the *Red Shirts* from the uniforms they wore.

In 1848, Garibaldi brought his Red Shirts back to the Italian peninsula. For many years Garibaldi and his small army fought battles against the Austrians and their allies. Finally he was defeated. Once again he escaped. This time he went to the United

Garibaldi and his Red Shirts fought to free and unite the states of Italy.

States. He raised money there to help his army. He waited for a chance to return to the Italian peninsula to lead his troops in the final battle for Italian unity.

The winning of Italian nationhood needed good political leaders as well as soldiers. Two of these political leaders were the king of Piedmont, Victor Emmanuel, and his clever prime minister, Camillo Cavour (kä mēl' lô kä vür'). Piedmont was one of the nine independent states of the Italian peninsula.

Piedmont had a constitution. It also had an elected parliament. Victor Emmanuel and Cavour worked hard to improve conditions in Piedmont. Under their leadership, the people built railroads. They improved farming and conditions in the factories. Soon Piedmont became an example for all the Italian states. It showed the people of these states that with a constitution and a parliament, many improvements in society could be made. Many Italians wanted Victor Emmanuel to be king of a united Italy. They believed that all of Italy could be governed as Piedmont was.

● Why were skilled statesmen as necessary as revolutionary leaders in the making of the nation-state of Italy? Do you think that such a combination is often needed in politics? Can you think of other examples? Explain

★ Find out more about the Red Shirts and Garibaldi. He led one of the most exciting lives in history.

The big problem remained. How could Austrian power be driven out of Italy? The little kingdom of Piedmont could not defeat Austria alone. Cavour persuaded Emperor Napoleon III of France to help by sending a French army. The French army helped to fight Austria. However, Napoleon III did not keep all his promises. France made peace with Austria before Italy was united and free. Cavour was so disappointed that he resigned as prime minister.

The small Piedmont army, with the help of France, had stood up to the Austrians. All over the peninsula the people began to follow Piedmont's example. The feeling of Italian nationalism was stronger than ever. Cavour returned to office. Garibaldi returned to Italy with his army of Red Shirts. Throughout Italy, people rose up in revolt against the Austrians. After several years of fighting, the dream of Italian unification came true. By 1870, the uniting of the Italian states was complete. The nation-state of Italy had been made. It had a monarch, a constitution, and an elected parliament.

The struggle for Italian unity was long and hard. Yet the controlling idea of nationalism helped the Italians form an independent nation-state.

WESTERN CONTROLLING IDEAS
SPREAD TO THE FAR EAST

By the end of the nineteenth century, many of the nation-states of Western Europe had built big industries. The merchants of these nations looked for new places to sell their manufactured goods. We have seen that they traded with people in the non-Western world. Sometimes they made trade agreements with non-Western governments. This meant that they would be allowed to trade their products freely with the people of these foreign countries. Sometimes Europeans became rulers of non-Western areas. The Europeans were able to control trade in these areas. In Chapters 2, 3, and 4, we saw the beginnings of Western imperialism. Let us now look at one example of Western imperialism at the end of the nineteenth century. This example is Western expansion into Japan.

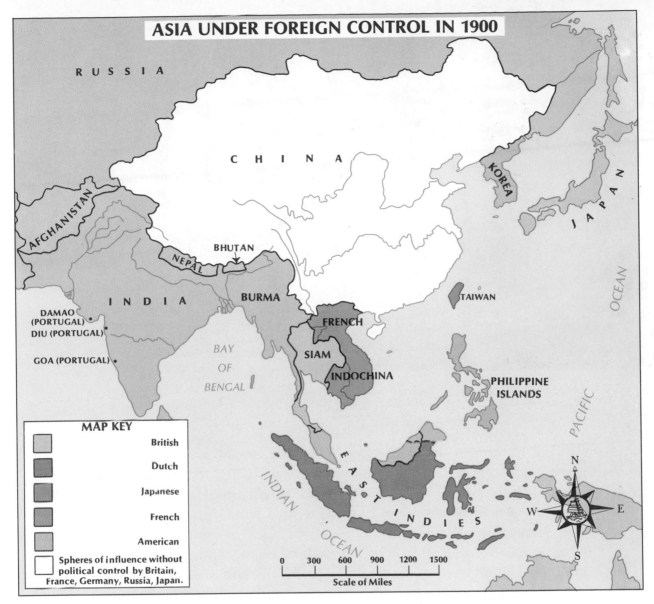

ASIA UNDER FOREIGN CONTROL IN 1900

MAP KEY

- British
- Dutch
- Japanese
- French
- American
- Spheres of influence without political control by Britain, France, Germany, Russia, Japan.

Scale of Miles

0   300   600   900   1200   1500

▶ Look at the map of Asia in 1900. Which European nations had influence in Asia? Which European nations had political control of Asian countries? Which countries? Where was there European economic control without political control?

Western Influence in Japan

In 1853, President Millard Fillmore of the United States of America sent a Navy Commodore, Matthew C. Perry, with a letter to the Japanese shogun. President Fillmore wanted to make trade agreements with Japan.

His suspicions aroused by Perry's arrival, the Japanese emperor had artists report on the actions of the foreigners. They sent him detailed sketches of the Commodore, his ship, and his party.

● What was the position of the shogun in Japan? What power did he have?

For over two hundred years Japan had closed itself off from the outside world. It did not allow trade with any nations. In fact Japan did not want to have anything to do with outsiders. Sometimes American ships went to trade with China, Japan's neighbor. Sometimes American whaling ships hunted whales in Japanese waters. When shipwrecked sailors were captured by the Japanese, they were often treated cruelly. By the 1850's, Americans were demanding protection for their sailors. They were also demanding that the Japanese let American steamships pick up fuel in Japanese ports. Most of all, the Americans wanted permission to exchange their goods for the treasures of Japan.

Commodore Perry anchored in Edo Harbor with four steamships under his command. He delivered President Fillmore's letter. He said that he would return the next year to get an answer to the president's letter.

How did the Japanese government receive President Fillmore's letter? The ruling shogun was weak. He knew that he was losing his power. He also knew that there were many people in Japan who wanted to open Japan for trade with the outside world. The shogun gave the letter to the emperor. The emperor and his advisors agreed to the requests of President Fillmore. Japan would allow the Americans to refuel their ships in Japanese ports. The Japanese promised better treatment of shipwrecked American sailors. They also agreed to allow limited trade with the United States. So Commodore Perry's voyage to Japan had helped to open the door which had been closed to the outside world for so long.

The American entry into Japan also caused many Japanese to feel a sense of nationalism. Many people in Japan were angry that foreigners were allowed to trade in Japan. They were unhappy with the weak government of the shogun. They felt he should have stood up against the Americans. Many Japanese took a new interest in the ancient Shinto beliefs. The idea that the emperor was the head of Shintoism and the ruler of the Japanese government again attracted them. The shogun was forced to resign. A new emperor, known as the Meiji (mā′jē) emperor, took over the leadership of the government. Like his proud people, Emperor Meiji wanted to make sure that Japan would never again give in to a foreign nation. He began to build up the armed forces of Japan. The army and navy were under his direct control.

- Was the anti-foreign attitude of many Japanese people nationalistic? Explain.

- How was the Shinto religion used for nationalistic purposes?

Like the Japanese emperors of the past, the Meiji emperor was thought to be a god. The Japanese believed his orders were the will of the gods. Yet even the emperor was influenced by the controlling ideas of the West. He sent his ambassadors to the countries of the West to see how these controlling ideas were at work. He became interested in the democratic type of government. The emperor did not really want democracy for Japan. But he wanted to try out certain ideas of the democratic governments in the West. The emperor decided to set up a representative assembly. Only a small percentage of the Japanese people could vote for members of the assembly. For the first time, however, some of the people in Japan had a small voice in Japanese government.

In the late 19th century, after many years of isolation, the Japanese opened their ports to American and European merchants. Westerners and Japanese gathered at these ports and exchanged ideas of cultures and technology.

The emperor convinced the Japanese people that they should learn all about the ideas of the Western world. He realized that the Western nations were strong. He wanted Japan to be a strong nation, too. He wanted Japan to be able to make the great advances in science and technology that the West had made. From the British the Japanese learned how to build railroads, set up a telegraph system, and organize the navy. French advisors helped the Japanese change their laws and organize their army. German doctors taught the Japanese about modern medicine and public health. Americans helped set up a public education system in Japan. Italians taught the Japanese about Western painting and sculpture. Under the Emperor Meiji, the Japanese began to catch up with the West. They were the first non-Western people to do this.

As the Japanese became more interested in commerce, their economy grew. Many big industrial cities grew up in Japan. Some of the fishing villages became important trade centers.

The life of the Japanese people also changed. The economy became more industrial. More people were needed to work in the factories. Agricultural machinery made it possible for fewer people to do the farming for Japan's food supply. More and more people left the farms and went to the cities to work in industry. As had happened in Europe, the old feudal system began to break down. Serfdom was ended by the government. Former serfs became owners of small areas of land.

In fifty years, the Japanese had learned many things from the West. They had changed their government, their economy, and their society. They had been affected by some of the controlling ideas of the West. Like nation-states of the West, they felt ready to expand. They soon began to do so.

- What elements in Japanese history and in the character of the Japanese people might explain their willingness to change?

- Had the Japanese ever before used foreigners to help them change their ways?

- Discuss the role played by the Japanese government in encouraging the Industrial Revolution in Japan. Did the English government use the same sort of planning to bring about the Industrial Revolution in Britain?

- In what ways does the geographic location of Japan remind you of the location of Britain?

- In what ways did Japan's reactions to the West save it from falling under foreign control? Explain.

★ From current news reports, find examples of Western influences on the Far East today.

chapter 7

Nationalism and Democracy in the New World

The first revolution for national independence began in 1776 in the New World. It was a revolution for self-government, too, and it led to democracy in the United States. From America, the idea of revolution spread to France, in 1789.

As we have seen, the ideas of nationalism and self-government spread through Europe. Then they moved to Japan. Later they spread all over Asia and Africa. They are still causing revolutions today.

However, long before these ideas reached Japan, they were carried through the whole of the New World. They brought independence to the Spanish and Portuguese colonies of Latin America. They brought self-government to Canada. They helped to cause a civil war in the United States.

- Why does the idea of nationalism often cause revolution or war?

- Why does the idea of democracy sometimes cause revolution?

- Why do the ideas of nationalism and democracy often go together?

- Why does a nationalist movement sometimes lead to dictatorship instead of democracy?

The American Civil War was a conflict between the ideas of nationalism and democracy.   129

The Colonies of Spain and Portugal

The empires of Spain and Portugal in the New World started in the sixteenth century. These empires included most of Central America, South America, and the Caribbean (kə rib'iən) Islands. They lasted until the early nineteenth century. Soon after 1800, a revolutionary movement for independence began in the Latin American colonies. To help understand this movement, we should learn what the colonies were like before 1800.

● What civilizations had existed in Latin America before the sixteenth century? What happened to these civilizations after the arrival of the Spanish?

★ What large country in South America today was once a Portuguese colony?

★ What treaty settled the rival colonial claims of Spain and Portugal? What were its terms?

Spain was the principal colonizer in Central and South America. The king of Spain sent governors, officials, and soldiers to rule its New World colonies. He sent churchmen to teach and convert the people. Settlers came to set up cotton and sugar plantations. At first, American Indians supplied the labor for these plantations. Later, African slaves were imported to work on the land and in the mines.

Laws for the Spanish colonies were made in Spain. They were carried out by Spanish officials. The settlers had no voice in their government. The colonies were not allowed to trade with each other. All the goods and raw materials of Latin America were sent to the mother country, Spain. The colonies remained underdeveloped. They had no industries of their own.

● What is this type of economic policy called?

► What other empires had similar economic policies?

Social classes were sharply divided in the Spanish colonies. The ruling group was the Spanish-born officials. These officials set the laws and controlled the wealth. Beneath them were the **creoles** (krē'ōlz). Creoles were descended from Spanish settlers.

They were often educated landowners. Still, they had no power in the colonial government. They resented being ruled by officials from Europe. The next group was made up of people with mixed Indian and European heredity. They were called **mestizos** (mes tē'zōs). The mestizos were looked down on by the creoles, although they had some land and wealth. At the bottom of society were the Indians and black slaves who worked the land.

By the end of the eighteenth century, the desire for freedom was strong in many parts of the world. Revolutions had taken place in France and the United States. These revolutionary movements had been caused in part by the ideas of the *Enlightenment*. People began to think about the *rights of man*. Many Latin Americans were eager to overthrow colonial rule. Feelings of nationalism grew. These feelings united people in the cause of freedom.

● What was the Enlightenment? What were its basic ideas?

Spain tried very hard to stop the spread of these ideas in its colonies. Books and newspapers were controlled by the government. People were not allowed to travel freely outside the continent. Even so, the ideas of the Enlightenment spread. Creoles who had been educated in Europe were eager to practice these ideas at home. They thought the rights of man were more impor-

Persons of mixed European and Indian heredity were looked down on by the descendants of the Spanish settlers.

tant than the rights of monarchs. They wanted to reshape and re-form their government. Books were smuggled into the Spanish colonies. This was done even at the risk of harsh punishment. Patriots met in secret to read and discuss them. Sometimes European goods that were shipped to Latin America came packed in old newspapers. Spanish officials often forgot to remove these wrappings. People eagerly read and shared the newspaper stories about the French and American Revolutions.

The Winning of Independence in the Spanish Colonies

In the early nineteenth century, Spain and Portugal were growing weak. In 1808, Napoleon invaded Spain. He placed his brother, Joseph Bonaparte, on the throne of Spain. This event gave Latin American patriots the chance to rebel. Joseph, a Frenchman, did not command the loyalty of the Spanish people, either in Spain or in Latin America. Napoleon's takeover greatly weakened Spanish influence in the colonies.

Popular rebellions broke out in Latin America. The independence movement produced two remarkable leaders. They were **Simón Bolívar** (sē mōn' bo lē'vär) and **José de San Martín** (hō say dā san mär tēn').

Simón Bolívar was a Venezuelan general. He became known as the "liberator of the north." Bolívar was a fiery soldier and a colorful patriot. Everywhere he went, he was hailed as the champion of freedom. Flowers were thrown before him. Fellow patriots eagerly joined his cause.

Bolívar led daring attacks on the royal armies of Spain. He defeated the enemy in Colombia, Panama, Venezuela, and Ecuador. He united these lands in a new republic which he named Great Colombia. Bolívar gained many honors and titles.

▶ Locate Great Colombia on the map on page 133. Why was Bolívar known as the "liberator of the north"?

José de San Martín became known as the "liberator of the south." He was quite different from Bolívar. He, too, was a great soldier. However, he did not seek any glory for himself. He was not interested in honors, titles, or gifts.

INDEPENDENCE OF SPANISH COLONIES IN LATIN AMERICA

MEXICO 1821

CUBA 1898

CENTRAL AMERICA 1823

PANAMA

VENEZUELA

GREAT COLOMBIA 1819

ECUADOR

PERU 1821

BOLIVIA 1826

PARAGUAY 1811

CHILE 1818

UNITED PROVINCES OF LA PLATA (ARGENTINA) 1816

GULF OF MEXICO

ATLANTIC OCEAN

PACIFIC OCEAN

ANDES MOUNTAINS

Spanish Colonies

0   500   1000   1500   2000
Scale of Miles

San Martín began his campaign in his homeland, Argentina. He freed Argentina and Chile from Spanish rule. He then set out to win independence for Peru. This was a more difficult task. Spanish power was still strong in Peru. Also, to enter Peru, San Martín's armies had to cross the Andes (an'dēz) Mountains.

► Locate the Andes on a map of South America. In which countries are they?

San Martín organized a fighting force to attack Peru. Many men volunteered to serve in his army. Women made uniforms and bandages for the soldiers. Many women sold their jewels to help pay for the campaign.

The march over the Andes was one of great suffering. After the Himalayas (him'ə lā'əz), the Andes are the highest mountains in the world. Many men died from cold and lack of oxygen.

● In what part of the world are the Himalayas?

Mule-drawn sleds carried cannon through the snowy mountain passes. Soldiers built bridges across the mountain streams.

The Spanish leaders did not know what route San Martín was taking. They scattered their armies too thinly. San Martín's forces were able to defeat the Spanish forces. Then San Martín occupied part of the country. However, the Spanish were still powerful in the highland. San Martín felt he could not drive them out of Peru without help. He asked Bolívar for aid.

Bolívar and San Martín met in Ecuador to plan their campaign. Their meeting was kept secret. No one knows exactly what took place at this historic meeting. However, the two great liberators could not agree to work together. Perhaps they had different ideas for the unification of South America. Perhaps they were unwilling to share power. In any case, San Martín left South America and never returned. He spent the rest of his life in France.

However, San Martín's army joined Bolívar's forces. Together, they completed the liberation, or freeing, of Peru. By 1824, all of Spain's Latin American colonies had been liberated.

▶ Look at the map on page 133 showing the dates of independence for the Spanish colonies. Locate the places that were important in the struggle for independence.

Problems of Independence

San Martín and Bolívar both realized that the Spanish colonies had very little experience in self-government. San Martín was afraid that a sudden change from the colonial system to democracy would not work. He wanted the colonies to be ruled as monarchies.

Bolívar hated the idea of monarchy. He wanted to set up a republican form of government in South America. However, he realized that a strong leader was needed to unite the people. Bolívar meant to be that leader. He thought democracy should come gradually, as people became prepared for self-government.

Some people were afraid that Bolívar would become a dictator and seize all power for himself. Moreover, other ambitious patriots were also eager to lead the new government. There were many plots against Bolívar. Many men distrusted him.

● Why did many people distrust Bolívar? What often happens when one man holds all the power?

The patriotic fighters had won their battle for freedom. However, they had very little experience in governing. Spain had not encouraged representative government in its colonies. It had not developed their economies. Laws favored the wealthy landowners. Judges were often corrupt. A few people were rich. A great many were poor. The wars of independence had ruined many farms and villages.

Quarrels broke out among the colonists. South America was divided. Governments were weak. Before long, Bolívar's union of Great Colombia fell apart.

As an old man, Bolívar gave up hope of uniting South America. He declared, "America is ungovernable. Those who have served the revolution have plowed the sea."

● What did Bolívar mean by this statement?

● Was the United States of America ever threatened with *disunion* after independence? Explain.

★ Find out how Mexico became independent. What part was played by Hidalgo (ē dal′gō), Iturbide (ē tür bē′dā), Santa Anna (sän′ta ä′nä), and Juarez (hwä′rās)?

The Independence of Brazil

For many years, Portugal paid little attention to Brazil. Brazil's wealth in lumber and minerals was undeveloped. Unlike Spain, Portugal did not establish a strong colonial government or a mercantilist trading system. Brazil had a small and scattered population. Two-thirds of the people were Indian and African slaves who worked on plantations. Tribes of Indians lived in the interior of the country, under very primitive conditions.

● Look at a physical map of Brazil. Give some reasons why it would be hard to settle and govern all of Brazil.

▶ Name another area where Europeans had difficulty in exploring and settling.

When Napoleon invaded Portugal in 1807, the king fled to Brazil with his family and court. King John decided to rule his empire from the New World. Fourteen years later, the king returned to Portugal. Napoleon had lost power. Portugal needed a king once again. However, Portugal had grown weak.

▶ Would a weakened empire be able to rule its colonies well?

King John left his son Pedro (pā drŭ) behind to rule in Brazil. Before he left, he said, "Pedro, Brazil will, I fear, ere long separate herself from Portugal. If so, place the crown on your own head rather than allow it to fall into the hands of adventurers."

King John's fears came true. The ideas of the Enlightenment spread to Brazil. As these ideas spread, a revolutionary movement grew. Pedro knew Portugal was not powerful enough to stop the drive toward freedom. So, he took his father's advice. He led the independence movement himself. In 1822, Brazil declared its independence from Portugal. Pedro became emperor of Brazil.

● Compare the independence movements in the Spanish colonies and Brazil. Did they share the same basic ideas? In what ways did these revolutions differ?

● Why did Pedro lead the independence movement in Brazil? What does this tell you about the force of the revolutionary movement in Latin America?

The independence movement had succeeded in the Americas. Most of Europe's former colonies were now independent nations. However, three great kingdoms in Europe wanted to see Latin America returned to Spain and Portugal as colonies. Russia,

Pedro II (right), the son of Brazil's first emperor, was the last monarch of the country. His reign (1840–1889) was an era of great social and industrial progress.

Prussia, and Austria formed the **Holy Alliance**. They believed in the *divine right of kings*. They did not want to see colonies break away from empires. Colonies meant wealth, markets, raw materials, and power for the mother country. The members of the Holy Alliance were willing to help Spain retake her colonies by force.

● Why did the European empires consider the independence movement a threat?

President James Monroe issued an important statement against the Holy Alliance. This was the **Monroe Doctrine**. The Monroe Doctrine stated that European nations must not interfere in New World affairs. The United States would look on any interference as an unfriendly act.

The Monroe Doctrine showed that the United States favored independent nations in Latin America. The United States was willing to go to war to protect their independence.

● What did the Monroe Doctrine show about the growth of the United States as an international power?

Latin America has had many wars and revolutions in its history. However, European powers have seldom taken sides in these conflicts.

Latin America was never unified as Bolívar and San Martín had hoped. The revolutionary movement died out in many places.

Let us think about some of the reasons for this. We have seen that the Spanish government did not prepare its colonies for independence. It kept the economy weak and undeveloped. It did not train or educate the people. When freedom came, most people were still poor and illiterate. It was hard to spread the ideas of nationalism and democracy among people who had never been outside their own villages. The leaders of the independence movement could not agree on the best way to unify the land.

● It is said that the Monroe Doctrine built a wall around the Western Hemisphere. What does the statement mean?

● Why did the United States believe that the continued independence of its neighbors was important?

★ Find out if the United States ever interfered in Latin American affairs. Report on relations between the United States and Mexico in 1846 or between the United States and Nicaragua in 1909.

★ Find out what is meant by the Good Neighbor Policy (introduced in 1933 by President Franklin D. Roosevelt). Find out what is meant by the Alliance for Progress (introduced in 1961 by President John F. Kennedy). Find out how the United States interfered in a Latin American country in 1965.

★ Compare the revolutionary movement in Latin America with the American Revolution. Use these ideas to help you: central government, rule of law, democratic ideals, federal system, growth of industry, strong economy, literacy.

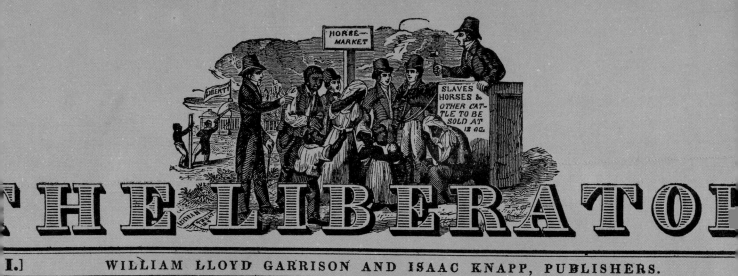

HORSE—MARKET

SLAVES HORSES & OTHER CAT-TLE TO BE SOLD AT 12 OC.

THE LIBERATOR

I.] WILLIAM LLOYD GARRISON AND ISAAC KNAPP, PUBLISHERS.

N, MASSACHUSETTS.] OUR COUNTRY IS THE WORLD—OUR COUNTRYMEN ARE MANKIND. [SATURDAY, APRIL

Nationalism, Democracy, and Humanitarianism in the United States

The controlling ideas of nationalism and democracy had been important in the making of the United States of America. Near the end of the eighteenth century, the United States of America had become a nation. The people of the United States made a constitution. Under this constitution, the states were united under a **federal, republican** system of government. This meant that the powers of government were divided between state governments and the national government. The national government and the state governments were based on the controlling idea of democracy. The people of the United States also had a feeling of nationalism that helped to keep them united.

- How might the federal system confuse people about nationalism and loyalty? Consider: Suppose the state of Virginia quarreled with the United States government. To which government should a Virginian be loyal? Suppose most of the people in Virginia voted for one thing, while most of the people in the whole United States opposed that thing.

Between 1820 and 1860 the United States became divided over a serious matter. This matter was slavery. Negro slaves had been brought from Africa. The southern parts of the United States depended on slave labor to grow cotton on the plantations.

However, humanitarian ideas were against slavery. All of the northern and most of the western states of the United States abolished slavery. Many American citizens also wanted to abolish slavery in the South. Or, at least, they wanted to stop slavery from spreading to new states in the West. Most white Americans in the southern states were angry at such interference with slavery.

● How were the controlling ideas of nationalism, democracy, and humanitarianism *dividing* the United States? Might the southerners want to form a separate nation? Might they want a democracy of their own instead of sharing that of the whole United States? Why?

The quarrel between the southern states and the rest of the United States grew bitter. *Should there be one or two nations of Americans?* The quarrel was complicated. It was not simply about ideas. It was also about economic interests. It was also a **culture conflict**—a battle between two ways of life. The way of life in the northern, free states was very different from the way of life in the southern, slave states.

▶ What is a *pluralistic* society?

● Would you say that the culture conflict in the United States came about because it had a pluralistic society?

Economic and Cultural Divisions

The Industrial Revolution had helped the North become an industrial area. Nearly all American industry and factories were located in the northern states. Big cities grew up in the North. These cities were industrial centers. Many people from Europe had come to America to work in the factories. They lived in the cities.

The economy of the South was agricultural, not industrial. The most important crop in the South was cotton. The factories of the North and factories in England bought large amounts of cotton. By 1860, the southern states depended on cash from the sale of their most important crop—cotton.

▶ Review the dangers of a one-crop economy.

A Southern cotton plantation   *A Northern industrial city*

The cotton growers depended on slave labor. Slaves from Africa planted and picked the cotton. In 1860, one out of four white southern families owned slaves. However, the economy of the southern states depended on large plantations. And there were many slaves on the large plantations.

- How did the northern and southern economic systems and ways of life differ?

The question whether slavery should be abolished divided northerners and westerners from southerners. By 1860, the North and the West had both cities and farm areas. In the farm areas, food crops were grown. Most of these crops were used in the North.

Railroads, by 1860, had begun to link the northern states with the western states and territories. They brought animals and grains from the West to the market centers of the Northeast. The railroads also carried the products of the northeastern factories to the West.

Even the society of the South was quite different from the society of the North and West. The wealthy men who owned large plantations formed a kind of aristocracy in the South. They were descended from English and French settlers. There were, in addition, many poor white people, as well as Negro slaves. Hardly any new immigrants came to the South from Europe. Thus, southern society was very different from that in the northern cities and villages and the western farms.

On top of these economic, social, and cultural differences came the quarrel over slavery.

Most northerners believed that slavery was wrong. Most southern plantation owners thought that slavery was necessary. Even white men who did not own slaves thought that Negroes should be kept in slavery. Many northerners wanted to force southern slave owners to give up their slaves. The southerners were determined to prevent the abolition of slavery. They even wanted to bring slavery into new western territories and states. Many northerners wanted to stop slavery from spreading.

● Defend the points of view of both southerners and northerners. Why would it be easier for northerners to be against slavery than it would for southerners? Why might a poor southern white who owned no slaves be in favor of slavery?

● What arguments would a humanitarian have against slavery?

► What other *abolitionist* movement have you read about?

The Coming of the Civil War

In 1860, the questions that divided northerners and southerners began to seem more and more important. In the minds of many northerners the question of slavery became a question of right and wrong, of good and bad. Many northerners wanted to force southerners to give up their slaves. Preachers gave sermons and said that all slave owners would go to hell. Books were published about the terrible conditions of slavery.

By the election of 1860, many southerners believed that only one course was open to them. They must **secede**, that is, separate themselves from the Union. They felt that they could protect their way of life only if they made an independent nation in the South.

In 1860, Abraham Lincoln was elected president of the United States. Lincoln was a lawyer from Illinois. He believed that slavery must not spread to new territories and states. Many southerners believed that President Lincoln would ruin the South. Even before Lincoln took office, seven southern states seceded from the Union.

THE SOUTHERN AND NORTHERN STATES DURING THE CIVIL WAR

MAP KEY
The Confederate States
The Union States
Territories

0 100 200 300 400 500
Scale of Miles

► Look at the map above. What is the name the southern states gave to their country after they had seceded from the Union?

● Are there any similarities between the South's view of its situation and the feelings among some of the nationality groups in Europe? Explain.

Does a state have the right to secede? The question had been argued for many years. Perhaps we can best see the arguments of both sides by reading the following statements.

Daniel Webster was a famous senator from a northern state. He believed that the people of the United States had created a union that was stronger than any simple agreement between states. In 1833 he said:

> . . . how can any man get over the words of the Constitution itself? —WE THE PEOPLE OF THE UNITED STATES DO ORDAIN AND ESTABLISH THIS CONSTITUTION. These words must cease to be a part of the Constitution . . . before any human ingenuity or human argument can remove the popular basis on which that Constitution rests, and turn the instrument into a mere compact between sovereign States.

Jefferson Davis, who became the president of the Confederate States of America in 1861, had an idea that was different from Webster's. He said in 1861:

> Our present political position . . . illustrates the American idea that governments rest on the consent of the governed, and that it is the right of the people to alter or abolish them whenever they become destructive of the end for which they were established.

- In your own words, tell what each statement means.

- Which statement is similar to the Declaration of Independence?

- Suppose the southern states were allowed to secede in 1860. What might happen to the remaining union of states if other disagreements arose in later years?

- To what do the words *union* and *confederate* refer? What does each word mean?

- What secession had happened earlier in the history of the United States?

When President Lincoln took office he was faced with the fact that seven southern states had seceded. What would he do? He believed that his most important work was to *save the Union*.

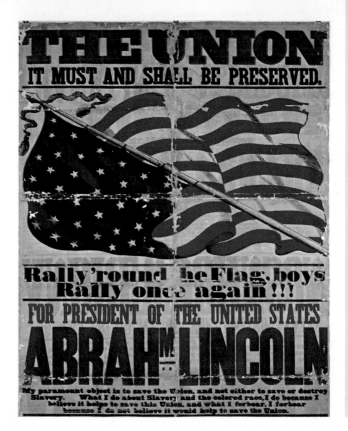

Many people wanted President Lincoln to abolish slavery. Let us
read part of Lincoln's answer to their questions.

> I would save the Union. I would save the Union in the
> shortest way under the Constitution. . . .
>   If I could save the Union without freeing any slave, I
> would do it — if I could save it by freeing all the slaves, I
> would do it — and if I could do it by freeing some and leaving
> others alone, I would also do that. . . . I have here stated
> my purpose according to my views of official duty; and I in-
> tend no modification of my oft-expressed personal wish that
> all men everywhere could be free.

- Which issue was more important to Lincoln as president — the future
  of the Union or the end of slavery?

- Do you think that Lincoln thought nationalism was important? Did he
  also believe in democracy?

- Did Lincoln believe slavery was wrong?

The people in both the North and the South were fearful of a war over the issue of secession. Each side began to arm. Both the North and the South were determined to protect their interests. On April 21, 1861, Confederate troops attacked Fort Sumter, a Union fort on the coast of South Carolina. Lincoln asked the men of the northern states to join the army of the Union. He wanted to save the Union even if the North had to go to war to do it.

The Confederate states formed an army, too. Four more southern states seceded. The people of the South were willing to fight a war to defend their right of secession. Soon the army of the Union was at war with the army of the Confederacy. This war is called the **American Civil War**.

★ Report on one or more battles of the Civil War.

The Course of the Civil War

Early in the war the Confederate States of America—or the Confederacy—was formed. Its capital was Richmond, Virginia. Jefferson Davis was its president.

The Civil War was cruel and destructive. Some of the men in the blue uniforms of the North were the cousins or even the brothers of the men in the gray uniforms of the South. Whole cities and great stretches of countryside were looted and burned.

At first, the army of the Confederacy was able to stop the Union troops from advancing into the South. Later, southern food supplies and ammunition began to run short. The factories of the northern cities were able to keep the army of the North supplied.

● How would you describe the *aims*, or *objectives*, of each side in the Civil War? Conquest of the other side? Making the other side get tired of fighting? National independence? National unity? Preserving slavery? Abolishing slavery?

The real turning point of the war came in July, 1863. The Confederate troops, under their great general Robert E. Lee, made an effort to invade the North. They met the Union forces at Gettysburg, Pennsylvania. There a gigantic battle took place. Losses on both sides were heavy. In the battle, 7,000 men died and 44,000 men were wounded. The southern forces were defeated. Southern spirit was weakened. Later, President Lincoln gave a famous speech at the cemetery at Gettysburg. He spoke not as the leader of the North alone, but as the president of the whole nation.

> Fourscore and seven years ago our fathers brought forth on this continent a new nation, conceived in liberty, and dedicated to the proposition that all men are created equal. Now we are engaged in a great civil war, testing whether that nation, or any nation so conceived and so dedicated can long endure. . . . .
>
> It is rather for us to be here dedicated to the great task remaining before us — that from these honored dead we take increased devotion to that cause for which they gave the last full measure of devotion — that we here highly resolve that these dead shall not have died in vain — that this nation, under God, shall have a new birth of freedom — and that government of the people, by the people, for the people, shall not perish from the earth.

● Notice that Lincoln did not say that the North must conquer and put an end to the South. He said that the very future of democratic government for the entire nation was at stake. Why might some southerners agree with Lincoln's words?

● Why did Lincoln's words make it easier for the southerners to accept defeat?

● Explain in your own words how Lincoln felt that democracy and nationalism were not able to be separated in the United States.

After the battle of Gettysburg, the South was fighting a losing war. In 1864, General Ulysses S. Grant became the commander of the Union forces. Under General Grant, the Union troops began winning important victories. They also weakened the South by destroying southern crops and property.

★ Report on Sherman's March through Georgia and the Carolinas.

During the war, most slaves had continued to work on the southern farms. As the war came to a close, more and more blacks joined the northern forces to help win the war. By the

Recruitment posters encouraged other blacks to join the Union army.

spring of 1865, the southern supplies were almost gone. Without supplies the army of the Confederacy could not last. General Lee lost more than half his men. The time to surrender had come. On April 9, 1865, Lee met Grant at Appomattox (ap'ə mat'əks) Court House in Virginia to sign a peace agreement.

In many ways, the years immediately after the war were as difficult as the war years. On April 14, 1865, President Lincoln was shot by a madman. Lincoln died the following day. The nation had lost its leader. But the Union had been saved, and slavery was ended by law.

We have seen how nationalism and democracy were tested in the United States by a great civil war. The Union survived. The ideas of nationalism and democracy were stronger than ever. Yet the problems of rebuilding the nation were great. In the end, the task was done, but the hatreds left by war and the evils left by slavery lasted. They are still to be found in the United States today.

- What hatreds and evils left by the war and slavery can you name?

- Do you think that the Civil War might have broken out if there had been no slaves? Explain. What, in your opinion, was the *main cause* of the war?

- If you had been an American statesman in the 1850's, what steps would you have recommended to avoid civil war?

- Does the American Civil War remind you of any problems in the independent nations of Latin America? What problems?

- Democracy was more popular in Europe after 1865 than it had been in 1861–1863. Why was this so?

★ Canada gained self-government under a federal system in 1867. Find out how this happened.

Controlling Ideas and the Interaction of Cultures

The American Civil War is perhaps the best example we can find of the great power of the ideas of nationalism, democracy, and humanitarianism. Both sides were fighting for their own type of nationalism and for the right to govern themselves. Humanitarian ideas on slavery brought the quarrel to a head.

After the Civil War, democracy and nationalism were more popular than ever in the West. They began to be popular in non-Western cultures, too. *Acculturation*, in non-Western countries, took the form of imitating Western ideas of nationalism and democracy. We have seen this happen in Japan. It also happened in India, in China, in the Arab nations, and, later on, in Africa and Southeast Asia.

Humanitarianism, too, had a victory in the American Civil War. Slavery was abolished in the United States. About the same time, serfdom was abolished in Russia. Soon after this, slavery was abolished in Brazil. Apart from certain parts of Africa and Arabia, slavery disappeared, for a time, from the world.

The nineteenth century set in motion many changes. Western ideas and Western imperialism influenced nearly every part of the world. The ideas of socialism and communism also became important to many peoples of the world. The interaction of cultures was far greater than ever before in the Human Adventure. What results would come from that interaction of cultures? We, who are alive today, are still seeing the results—both good and bad. Indeed, some results cannot yet be seen or foreseen. When ideas from different cultures mix, new patterns of history are made. That is what makes the story of mankind such a big and exciting adventure.

conclusion

Looking Back and Looking Forward

How many changes we have seen as we studied the Human Adventure! Some of the changes were great steps forward for man. They were changes that were never reversed. Agriculture, cities, writing, mathematics: these steps forward came in the period of ancient history. The classical period also saw steps forward. Great religions and philosophies appeared at the beginning of and during this period. In Greece and Rome we saw political experiments—democracy and republic—that men have never forgotten. During the Middle Ages came important steps in technology: gunpowder, optics, printing, stronger ships. In the Modern Age still more big steps forward were made. Natural science grew swiftly. The whole world was explored. Nations with

Modern artists have adopted new ways to depict traditional subjects.

representative governments came into being. The Industrial Revolution changed men's ways of life as much as the discovery of agriculture had changed them 8,000 or 9,000 years earlier.

Some changes were not like these great steps forward, but they were very important. These were the changes that brought many different cultures into being. We have seen a few of these cultures. There were the Middle Eastern cultures of ancient and medieval times: Sumer, Babylon, Egypt, and the Hebrew and Muslim Arab cultures. There were the cultures and civilizations of Africa. There were the Chinese and Indian cultures. In the Americas, Indian cultures grew. Some were civilized—the Maya, Inca, Aztec and others. Many others did not become civilizations. In Europe, many culture groups came into being.

In addition to these, there were thousands and thousands of changes that were part of the ebb and flow of human history. It is not easy to explain these changes. Why should a great empire rise and then fall? Why did barbarians attack civilized societies? Why did civilized societies grow weak? Why did some societies become feudal? Why did monarchies and nations appear? Why did (and do) human societies go to war?

Historians have tried to see a pattern in such changes. They do not, however, agree on the pattern. Yet we can learn something about men—and about ourselves—as we study these zig-zag movements of history. Men are restless creatures. They experiment. They try to solve problems. They want things. They try to get power or wealth or knowledge. They can be kind. They can be cruel. They can be reasonable. They can also be very unreasonable.

Studying the Human Adventure, then, helps us to understand ourselves. History is a laboratory where social science can test its ideas.

- Would you say that the Human Adventure is a story of human *progress*? Explain.

- Give some examples from the Human Adventure of *steps backward*. Were these backward steps later recovered?

- What is your own idea about human nature? How does the Human Adventure support your idea?

● How can history help you test social science ideas like these?
   Absolute or *unlimited government* is unjust. (Political science)

   To have a high standard of living people need *capital* and the *division of labor*. (Economics)

   Societies are usually divided into *classes*. The classes may fight for power. (Sociology)

   The *controlling ideas* of a society will tell you much about its *culture* and about the way its people behave. (Anthropology)

★ Think of some more social science ideas that can be tested in the laboratory of history.

The World in 1900

Our studies have brought us to the end of the nineteenth century. It is a good place to pause. The next step of the Human Adventure takes us into the quite different world of the twentieth century.

Perhaps the most striking thing about the world in 1900 was **optimism** (op'tə miz əm). Optimism means the feeling that things are fine, and that they will surely get even better. The opposite of optimism is **pessimism** (pes'ə miz əm). Most people in Western Europe and in the United States were full of optimism. They believed that their culture was the best in the world. They believed it was strong enough to lead all people to a better life.

Everywhere new industries would raise the standard of living. Hunger would disappear. So would ignorance. There would be no more big wars. Everywhere men would learn about democracy. Absolute governments would be things of the past.

Why should these good things not happen? Look how far Western Europe had moved forward in the nineteenth century! Germany and Italy were now nation-states making great progress. Japan, which was copying Western ideas, was an industrial country with an elected parliament. Africa had been explored and opened up to trade. New English-speaking nations had gained independence, just as the United States had done. These nations were Canada, Australia, and New Zealand. Old, absolute governments still ruled in China and Russia, but it looked as if they would not last long.

Since Napoleon there had been no world wars. The bloodiest war of the century had been the American Civil War. The Civil War had proved two things. It had proved that slavery could no longer exist in civilized societies. It had proved, too, that a representative democratic government was as strong in putting down rebellion as any absolute government.

There had been many short wars. They had mainly been limited wars. **Limited wars** are wars fought to gain a limited goal. The opposite of limited war is **total war**—war to conquer the enemy completely. Limited wars are usually less terrible than total wars. Many of the wars of the nineteenth century were short imperialist or anti-imperialist struggles.

● Why are limited wars usually less terrible than total wars?

★ Look up one or more of the limited wars of the nineteenth century. For example: the Crimean (krī mē′ an) War, the war in northern Italy in 1859, the Seven Weeks' War between Austria and Prussia in 1866, the Franco-Prussian War of 1870–71, the Spanish-American War of 1898.

Thus the wars of the nineteenth century were mainly small ones. People hoped that the **great powers** had learned how to respect international law. They hoped, too, that they had learned how to keep the balance of power. If these things had been learned, there need be no more terrible total wars.

● What is the *balance of power?* How does keeping the balance help to prevent great wars?

Another thing that encouraged optimism was the spread of education in the West. In most Western countries most grown men could vote to elect representatives. In order to vote, they needed to know about politics. Many men had to do skilled work. In order to do this work they needed to read, write, and use figures. Therefore, in all Western nations, education for everyone began to be the rule. More and more Western nations had public school systems. More people could read and write than ever before in the Human Adventure.

Because so many people could read, newspapers became popular. Everyone who wanted to could read about the govern-

MAN'S ROAD TO PROGRESS

ment. He could read about things that had happened only a few hours before. He could read about them even if they had happened 10,000 miles away. News traveled fast by cable and telephone.

These new things ought to help people make sensible judgments in politics and in economics. At least, that is what many people thought. Surely, they said, governments are going to be better than they ever could be in the past.

When they thought of invention and industry, too, people in 1900 were full of optimism. Electrical power would give men more goods and services than ever before. Railroads and steamships carried food, manufactured goods, and people to most inhabited areas. Motorcars were already working well. In 1900, the first airship with engines was built by Count von Zeppelin (fôn zep' ə lən). In 1895, an Italian, Marconi (mär kō' nē), invented radio. In the same year, X-rays were discovered. These rays were only one of many medical discoveries that promised better health for everyone.

It was truly a time of optimism. The changes that began with the rise of the West and the Modern Age had opened up new ways of living. Surely, most people believed, things would become better and better, for more and more people.

- Many of the changes we have been looking at were revolutionary. What were the major revolutions of the Modern Age? How would you describe them— *political, economic, intellectual,* or *social*?

- How had each revolution influenced the lives of ordinary people in the West? How had they influenced the lives of non-Western people?

- What challenges or problems do revolutions bring? Might revolutionary change make some people *pessimistic*? Explain.

Some Things That Did Not Change

Important parts of the civilization of 1900 were older than what we call the Modern Age. In the Human Adventure, some things are **permanent**—that is, they do not change at all or change only slowly. Among these things are *moral beliefs*, some *social customs*, and great *literature*.

The religions of 1900 were far older than the Modern Age. Europe remained mainly Christian. Christianity and Judaism went over the oceans to the Americas and wherever else Europeans settled. Africa remained Muslim in the north, and much of central and southern Africa remained pagan, although Christianity followed European exploration of Africa. Islam was the main religion of southwestern Asia. Most Indians remained Hindus or Muslims. Many Chinese remained disciples of Confucius. Buddhism was the religion of many peoples in southeastern Asia and Japan. The religious and moral beliefs of most people in 1900 had not been swept away by the Modern Age.

The literature of the people of 1900 was not all new. The famous writers of Greek and Roman and medieval times still were read by most educated people in Europe and America. The literature of the Muslim, Indian, and Chinese cultures still thrilled millions of men and women.

In 1900, the social ways of most countries owed much to the distant past. Even though political revolutions had overthrown some old governments, traditional ideas of order and justice and freedom lived on. The British political system had grown out of many centuries of national experience. The American political system was founded partly on British experience and partly on the ideas and institutions of old Greece and Rome. The French Revolution had shaken governments in Europe, but after that Revolution many of the old political patterns had risen up again.

Nearly everywhere in 1900, courts of law and ideas of justice that were much older than the Modern Age still kept peace among men. In the many new cities that grew up during the Industrial Revolution, the family remained the basic unit of society. Schools and universities had existed well before the Modern Age. The schools and universities of 1900 taught about older ideas as well as about the new knowledge of modern times.

In the West, men and women were better off and better educated than most men and women of earlier ages. But human beings in 1900 were not a new race of people. In the West, they had inherited the Jewish knowledge of God's ways toward man, the Greek understanding of human nature, the Roman ideas of law and order, and the Christian creed of faith, hope, and charity.

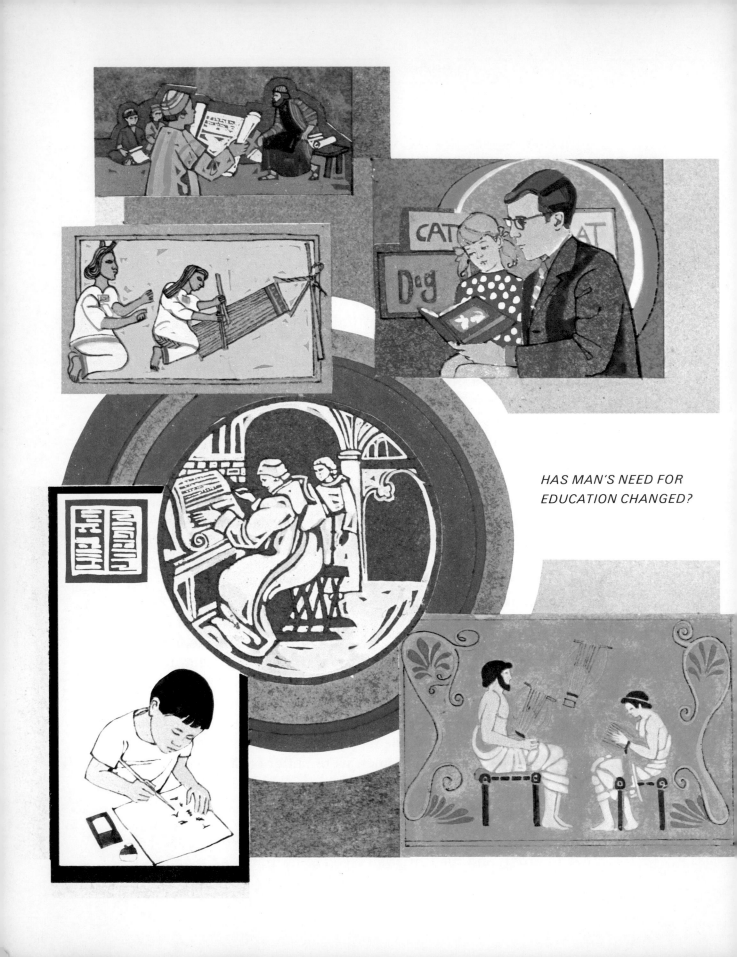

HAS MAN'S NEED FOR EDUCATION CHANGED?

The people of London, in 1900, were not more intelligent than the people of Athens had been, five centuries before Jesus was born. The people of Paris, in 1900, were not more patriotic than the old Romans had been. The people of New York, in 1900, were not more hard-working than the people of medieval Venice had been. Most of the people of 1900 still lived by old and tried beliefs. These people were not more human, or less human, than the folk of ancient Egypt and Sumer had been 5,000 years earlier.

The links in culture between one generation and the next, or between one age and the next age, make up what we call **social continuity**. The Human Adventure is a continuing adventure. Things done and thought in the past *continue* to have influence in our own time. Only human beings have social continuity. Human beings pass on knowledge and belief and art and custom from year to year. So we say that there is a *continuity* of laws, of skills, of beliefs. This continuity gives society a long, continuous life.

If we did not have that continuity, every new generation of people would be ignorant. A teacher of the Middle Ages said that the men of his time were like dwarfs standing upon the shoulders of giants. By "giants," he meant the wise men who lived in the past. Modern people know more than their ancestors. But they know more only because they have gained knowledge from earlier generations. If we did not inherit much wisdom and knowledge from our ancestors, we would know next to nothing.

So the Western and non-Western civilizations of 1900 were built upon many ancient ideas and customs and ways of living in a community. The mighty changes in the world after the year 1500 certainly had improved human life in some ways. Possibly they had injured human life in other ways. But those changes had not changed human nature. Nor had they destroyed everything that mankind had learned earlier.

● Why is it important to remember that certain things about human beings do not change, or change very slowly? What mistakes may be made by people who think that the knowledge of the past is useless? What mistakes may be made by a person who thinks it possible to change all human beings into perfectly "good" people?

● Discuss the idea that great moral values do not change, but that men's ways of using those values change from one culture to another and may change from one period to another. For example: would any reasonable person say that *cowardice* is better than *courage*? But the question then arises: What is the cowardly action in *this particular situation*? Is it cowardly to turn to a law court when someone has hurt or damaged you? Would it be braver to fight a duel with him? There have been times in history when most men would have said that the test of courage was a duel! Think of some other examples.

Looking Forward into the Twentieth Century

Was the optimism of men in 1900 well founded? Up to a point it was. Yet it was also badly mistaken. Progress—change for the better—was not as simple as many people thought.

Does this 20th-century painting give you a feeling of optimism or pessimism?

The optimists of 1900 thought, for instance, that soon democracy would be adopted everywhere. They believed that good political constitutions and sound representative government would be set up in every country. They trusted that great wars would never again happen. Even small limited wars would grow fewer and fewer.

And yet the optimists of 1900 were only fourteen years away from a terrible total war. When the First World War came, international order was blown apart. Dictators and men of violence rose to power in many societies. After 1914, nations that had been moving toward constitutional government and democratic ways turned back to tyranny. Countries that had known freedom and democracy for a century or more found it hard, after 1914, to keep their old principles of order, justice, and freedom.

The optimists of 1900 thought, too, that future generations everywhere would be even better fed, better housed, and better clothed than the people of the West were then. They thought that all nations would share in prosperity.

They could not know that during the next half-century there would be two great wars. These wars brought misery and poverty to many millions of human beings. After those wars, much of the West recovered its wealth. But a large part of the world grew poorer, not richer. In India, China, the East Indies, Latin America, and other lands, population increased more rapidly than the supply of food. Many countries experienced social and political revolutions. These revolutions set back the chances of economic growth.

The optimists of 1900 believed, besides, that people everywhere would grow more law-abiding. People would become gentler and more charitable. Life everywhere would be safer from violence or tyranny. Yet international law became less respected. Inside many states, justice was hard to find. Crimes increased in modern cities. Sometimes criminals seized power even in advanced countries.

In the twentieth century, a host of new challenges had to be faced. We have just been looking at a few of them: world wars, tyranny, crime, and the population explosion. There are others. Nuclear weapons may destroy the human race. Industry pollutes our air and waters. Hatred between Western and non-Western peoples may grow worse and worse. So may hatred between different races of mankind.

These are some of the challenges we shall study when we turn to look at our own century. The twentieth century seems to mark a new stage in the Human Adventure. Many historians think that a new period of history started about 1940 or 1950. Who knows? What will it be called?

The optimists of 1900 were wrong in their vision of the big social changes of the twentieth century. Yet they were right in many of their ideas about changes in knowledge and industry. Science has made and still makes great strides forward. So does medicine. So does the production of goods. In most Western societies, ordinary people enjoy a standard of living much higher than that of a king or nobleman three hundred years ago! In these societies, too, every young person has the chance—if he tries hard—to have the amount of education that only one or two people in a thousand could have had a hundred years ago. In Western societies, ordinary people have immense power in their hands. They have cars with as much power as a hundred horses. They have electrical machines in their homes that do more work than ten servants could have done a hundred years ago. As a result, many people have as much leisure as the wealthiest persons had in the past.

The question is: have we learned to use our power sensibly? Have we learned how to get the best out of education? Have we learned how to enjoy our leisure? The old unchanging things are still important. Understanding the good life, justice, social customs, great literature and art may be more necessary today than ever before.

Beyond Western societies, lies the non-Western world. Most non-Western people are not sharing the benefits of our "new" civilization. From the beginning of the Human Adventure this problem has come up again and again. In the past it brought destructive wars between civilized peoples and barbarians. These struggles caused, in part, the ebb and flow of civilization. Do we, today, know enough to cope with this new example of the age-old problem? That is the last and toughest question of all.

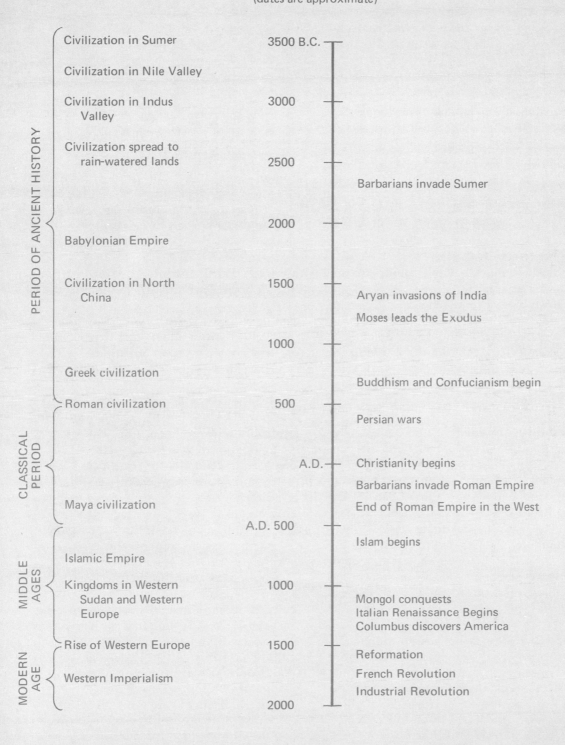

TIME LINE OF CIVILIZATION
(dates are approximate)

PERIOD OF ANCIENT HISTORY

Civilization in Sumer — 3500 B.C.

Civilization in Nile Valley

Civilization in Indus Valley — 3000

Civilization spread to rain-watered lands — 2500

Barbarians invade Sumer

2000

Babylonian Empire

Civilization in North China — 1500

Aryan invasions of India

Moses leads the Exodus

1000

Greek civilization

Buddhism and Confucianism begin

Roman civilization — 500

CLASSICAL PERIOD

Persian wars

A.D. — Christianity begins

Barbarians invade Roman Empire

Maya civilization

End of Roman Empire in the West

A.D. 500

MIDDLE AGES

Islam begins

Islamic Empire

Kingdoms in Western Sudan and Western Europe — 1000

Mongol conquests
Italian Renaissance Begins
Columbus discovers America

MODERN AGE

Rise of Western Europe — 1500

Reformation

Western Imperialism

French Revolution

Industrial Revolution

2000

GLOSSARY

Some words have many meanings. This list gives only the meanings of the words as they are used in this book. To find other meanings of these words, look them up in a dictionary.

abolitionist movement: a movement by those who wished to put an end to slavery.

acculturation: the results of adopting the culture features of another group.

American Civil War: the American war between North and South, from 1861–1865; often called the War Between the States.

annex: to join or add one thing to something larger.

anthropologist: one who specializes in anthropology, the scientific study of man's origins and development.

aristocracy: in the South, a group of people considered the upper class of society, primarily because of wealth.

bakunga: important Ganda chiefs who governed the largest land districts of Buganda.

bataka: heads of clans, who governed land belonging to their clans. They were lesser Ganda chiefs, ranking beneath the bakunga.

batangole: the Ganda king's trusted followers, who acted as a royal guard.

Bolívar, Simón: Venezuelan statesman, leader of the revolt against Spanish rule.

capitalist: one who uses money or property (capital) to make more money.

caste system: in Brahmanism and Hinduism, the social classes into which most people are born and in which they stay all their lives.

colonization: setting up a colony or community of people in a new land. The people live in a new place, but they keep their ties with their mother country.

communism: a system under which most or all property is owned by the state or community as a whole and is supposed to be shared by all.

Confederacy: the Confederate States of America.

Congress Party: the main political party in India. See Indian National Congress.

conquest and rule: a form of imperialism in which the conquering country governs, taxes, and trades with the inhabitants of the conquered country.

constitutional monarch: a ruler whose power is limited by a constitution.

controlling ideas: ideas that control or guide the way a person acts.

creoles: descendants of Europeans in Spanish America or the West Indies.

crown colony: a colony that does not have its own constitution or representative government; the ruler (or rulers) of the parent country controls legislation and administration in the crown colony.

cultural imperialism: a state where the culture of the imperial power has affected the native culture.

culture conflict: a struggle between peoples having different ideas and values.

culture contact: the meeting of people and ideas from different cultures; the things that happen when one culture or way of life comes into close touch with another and different culture.

currency: money in actual use in a country: paper, gold, silver, etc.

democracy: a system of government in which all the people share in the government of their society.

democratic socialism: a gradual and peaceful change from capitalism to socialism by democratic means.

direct democracy: a form of government in which the supreme power is in the control of the people and carried out by them directly, as in the Greek city-states.

dominance: rule; control.

economic imperialism: a state where the imperial power does not conquer or govern but uses its power to force a country to trade with it.

federal republican government: a republic where power is in the hands of the central and state governments.

fortified: made strong; protected against attack.

genocide: the planned killing of a people and their culture.

gold outflow: the leaving of gold from a country, usually from the treasury of the country, so quickly as to put a strain on the economy of that country.

great powers: those nations of the world that have the greatest political influence, resources, and military strength.

Hinduism: an Indian religion and way of life that shares several ideas with Buddhism. One who believes in Hinduism is called a Hindu.

Holy Alliance: a league formed by the leading rulers of Europe in order to prevent revolutions.

humanitarianism: love for one's fellow men and concern for their well-being.

ideology: a plan to remake or reshape society.

imperialism: extension of control of one people over another.

Indian independence: freedom from the control and influence of Great Britain.

Indian Mutiny (1857–59): the Sepoy Rebellion, when Indian soldiers in the British army fought against the British in India. As a result, India was governed by the Crown rather than by the British East India Company.

Indian National Congress: Indian political party founded by an Englishman, Allan Hume, who wished for a more representative form of government for the peoples of India; also called Congress Party.

indirect rule: an informal arrangement where one country advises another country or government, which automatically accepts the advice; ruled through native rulers.

interaction of cultures: the effect of action of one culture upon another.

kabaka: king of the Ganda who ruled for life and who had absolute rule over his people.

katikkiro: prime minister to the kabaka.

kowtow: the Chinese custom of kneeling and touching the ground with one's forehead to show respect to the emperor.

Liberia: country on the west coast of Africa colonized with freed American Negro slaves.

limited war: a war with an objective less than the total defeat of the enemy's forces.

literature: writings of a period or of a country, especially those kept alive by their beauty of style or thought.

Manchu: a member of a Mongolian people inhabiting Manchuria. Mongol tribes that helped the Ming emperor's forces to put down Chinese rebels. These tribes stayed in China and founded the Manchu dynasty.

means of production: everything necessary to produce things: land, factories, tools.

mestizo: in Spanish America, one who has Spanish and American Indian blood.

middleman: a trader or merchant who buys goods from the producer and sells them, usually at a profit, to another merchant or directly to the user.

Ming dynasty: the dynasty that ruled China from 1368 to 1644. It is said to be the last dynasty of true Chinese origin.

Mogul Empire: the Mongol conquerors of India who ruled from 1526 to 1857. They were Muslim Turks.

Monroe Doctrine: U.S. President James Monroe's warning to European nations against interference in the affairs of American nations.

moral beliefs: one's ideas of right and wrong, good and bad.

Muslim League: a political party formed by Muslims in India to work for Muslim rights and representation in government.

nationalism: a feeling of loyalty, pride, and patriotism toward one's nation-state.

Open Door: the policy of admitting all nations to a country on equal terms, especially for trade.

open ports: a port open to foreign trade. After losing the Opium War, China was forced to declare five cities as open ports. In these cities foreigners lived under the laws of their own countries.

opium: a habit-forming drug, used to ease pain. When taken habitually, it damages the mind and body.

opium trade: the practice of exchanging opium, rather than currency, for Chinese goods.

Opium War (1839–42): a war between China and Great Britain over illegal sale of opium to the Chinese.

optimism: the feeling that everything is fine or good and will get even better.

outmarry: to marry outside one's own clan. The Ganda could not marry anyone from their mother's or father's clan.

permanent: lasting for a long time, with little or no change.

pessimism: tendency to look on the dark side of things or to see difficulties and disadvantages, the opposite of optimism.

pluralistic: consisting of more than one element. In a pluralistic society, people with different cultures live side by side.

polygyny: the practice of having more than one wife at a time.

protectorate: a land under the protection of an imperial power that defends the land (protects it from other powers) in return for taxes and trade.

radicals: those who believe that society should be changed completely and quickly, using violence if it becomes necessary.

representative constitutional republic: a nation in which the citizens elect representatives to manage the government under a constitution which limits power and gives equality to all.

San Martín, José de: South American soldier and statesman.

secede: withdraw formally from an alliance or organization.

segregation: separation from others: e.g., people of a weaker culture are forced to live separated from the people of the dominant culture.

sepoy: an Indian soldier trained and equipped by the East India Company to fight alongside the British in India.

Sepoy Rebellion: British-trained Indian soldiers fought against British soldiers in India. See Indian Mutiny.

Seven Years' War: a European war fought from 1756 to 1763. This war laid the foundations of the British Empire because, at its end, French domination in Canada and French influence in India were ended.

Sierra Leone: a republic in western Africa, a member of the British Commonwealth. Many freed Negro slaves from the Americas moved to Sierra Leone.

Sinkiang: the westernmost province of China. Mongol land added to the Chinese Empire under Ch'ien Lung, the second great Manchu emperor, and colonized by the Chinese.

social continuity: the passing on of all that has been learned from one generation to the next.

social customs: long-established habits often having the force of law.

socialism: the idea that the interests of the community are more important than the interests of the individual; a plan for greater public control of property, business, and industry.

sociologist: one who is skilled in sociology, the scientific study of human society—how it developed, how it is organized, and how it functions.

sphere of influence: an area in which one nation has great political influence and special rights and power.

status: a state or condition of affairs; one's place in society.

subculture: a social group that exhibits character patterns which distinguish it from others within a larger culture or society.

total war: a war with the objective of total defeat of the enemy's armed forces.

totem: a natural object taken as the emblem of a tribe, clan, or family.

trading forts: a trading post that could be defended against an enemy.

treaty: an agreement between nations.

unequal treaty: a treaty between nations where a defeated country must accept terms that are harsh and often unfair.

Westernized: made western in ideas, character, ways, etc.

Will of Heaven: in Confucianism, a great spirit of wisdom and goodness that favors only a good ruler.

Yuan dynasty: the second of the early modern dynasties following the Sung dynasty. This dynasty lasted from 1260 to 1368.

INDEX